Of the few facts known about the life of GAIUS VALERIUS CATULLUS even his dates of birth and death are uncertain, but he was probably born in 84 B.C. The son of a wealthy citizen of Verona, either he or his family owned a villa on Lake Garda, but in Poem 68 he describes Rome as his home and says that his life was passed there. He writes as a friend of Cicero and other leading figures and appears as a leader of the new movement in poetry and a lover of the notorious Clodia Metelli, who was probably the Lesbia of the poems. In 57 he travelled as one of C. Memmius Gemellus's suite to Bithynia, where he visited his brother's grave. He started writing in 69 or 68 but, after his death in about 54 B.C., his work was all but lost for a thousand years.

PETER WHIGHAM is self-educated and, since his first job as a gardener in the Wye Valley, has been successively a schoolmaster, an actor in provincial repertory, a reporter for a mid-Wales newspaper, a school-master again, and a free-lance script writer for the B.B.C. In the early sixties he moved to Italy to devote himself entirely to writing. Largely as a result of his Catullus translations he was invited to give courses in verse composition at the University of California, where he stayed for two years. He now lives in the East Bay area of San Francisco. His most recent publications include *The Blue Winged Bee* (Poetry Book Society Choice for Spring 1969) and *ASTAPOVO or What We Are To Do*, both from Anvil Press Poetry, London. Peter Whigham's *The Poems of Catullus* has also been published in a bilingual edition by the University of California Press.

THE POEMS OF
CATULLUS

TRANSLATED WITH AN
INTRODUCTION BY
PETER WHIGHAM

PENGUIN BOOKS

Penguin Books Ltd, Harmondsworth, Middlesex, England
Penguin Books, 625 Madison Avenue, New York, New York 10022, U.S.A.
Penguin Books Australia Ltd, Ringwood, Victoria, Australia
Penguin Books Canada Ltd, 2801 John Street, Markham, Ontario, Canada L3R 1B4
Penguin Books (N.Z.) Ltd., 182–190 Wairau Road, Auckland 10, New Zealand

—

First published 1966
Published in Penguin Books 1966
Reprinted 1969, 1971, 1974, 1977

—

This translation and introduction copyright © Peter Whigham, 1966

—

Made and printed in Great Britain
by Richard Clay (The Chaucer Press) Ltd,
Bungay, Suffolk
Set in Monotype Bembo

CONTENTS

ACKNOWLEDGEMENTS

SOME of the poems originally appeared in *Artisan*, *The National Review*, *Agenda* and *Arion*, to whose editors I am indebted for permission to reprint them. Some also appeared in *Clear Lake Comes from Enjoyment*, Neville Spearman, 1959. Poem 61 was first printed in *The Marriage Rite*, The Ditchling Press, 1960. Both these books were written in collaboration with Denis Goacher.

In the specialised field of Catullan studies my debts are too widespread and diverse to be easily enumerated here. I can only hope that the book itself may in some sort prove a recompense for what I have pillaged from those more learned than myself. Unfortunately, C. J. Fordyce's *Catullus* (1961) did not appear until my work was more than half completed, but I have made what use of it I could. Burton and Smithers' curious but stimulating volume has been with me from the time when I began to make my first versions. Munro's *Criticisms and Elucidations of Catullus* (1878) and Robinson Ellis's Oxford Text, together with his *Commentary on Catullus* (2nd edn., 1889), have been my principal guides textually and exegetically. I have also used the texts of S. G. Owen (1893), Arthur Palmer (1896) and J. P. Postgate (1889). Mueller's text (1885) is of course incorporated in the Burton and Smithers volume. Salvatore Quasimodo's selected translation and Carlo Saggio's complete one have been an invaluable stimulus. I have also been helped by Ferrero's two studies (both Turin, 1955) and, perhaps most of all, by Noel's two-volume work: *Catulle* (An. XI – 1803), a fund of Renaissance and post-Renaissance lore on the subject of Catullus. From Landor's work as a

whole, and the second volume of his *Longer Prose Works*
(Crump, edn. 1893) in particular, I have derived valuable,
if somewhat idiosyncratic, insights. Finally, there has been
my old edition (1797) of Lemprière, and Carnevale's
Roma Nel IIIe Secolo (1896).

A year or so before his death, William Carlos Williams
had some of these poems read to him. He handed them
around among his friends. Not only his example as a poet
but this practical encouragement of his as a master was a
great help to me at a time when the book might well have
been left in an incomplete state: '*hoc tibi, quod potui, con-
fectum carmine munus/ pro multis, Alli, redditur officiis. . .*'.

Wine stains the verse;
the curse of time obliterates the arrogant line.

Then, in Verona, Campesani knows
the 'Roman hand':
"One woman could command
this song."
              He sang
and fourteen hundred years
later, it reappears –
              in the barrel's bung
(the hand that Campesani knows)
codex from wine-bung springing,
as from the dung
              – the rose.

WE know very little about Catullus's life: even the dates of his birth and death are uncertain. The likeliest figures are: born 84, died 54 B.C. His full name was Gaius Valerius Catullus. His father was a citizen of Verona and apparently of sufficient eminence to entertain Julius Caesar in his house. Either Catullus, or his family, owned a villa on the Sirmio peninsula on Lake Garda, about thirty miles west of Verona. We do not know where Catullus had his schooling, nor anything about his family, except that he had a brother who died before him. In poem 68 he tells us that already, at the age of 15 or 16, he had had his first experiences of love and, by implication, of poetry. In the same poem he describes Rome as his home and says that his life is passed there. We do not know when he left Verona, nor when he arrived in Rome nor where he lived when he was there. He speaks of a villa near Tivoli, but he must have had a town house as well. He constantly complains of being short of money, although he never seems wholly serious about this. He writes as a friend of Cicero and of many of the most distinguished figures of his day. He displays an aversion – again, less than completely serious – for Caesar and various members of his faction. He appears as one of the lovers of the notorious Clodia Metelli, and a leading figure – perhaps *the* leading figure – in the new movement in poetry. Sometime before 57 or 56 B.C. his brother must have died and been buried in the Troad, for it was in 57 that he, and probably his friend Gaius Cinna, accompanied C. Memmius Gemellus to Bithynia as members of his suite, and, according to the evidence of poem 101, Catullus paid a visit to his brother's grave when he was out there. A governor's term of office normally lasted a year, which means that poem 46 can be placed in the following spring when, if poem 4 is to be taken literally, Catullus returned to Italy in his own yacht, one that he had either bought, or perhaps had made, for the occasion. He appears to have sailed up the Adriatic and thence up the Po and the Mincio, or the Adige, to within a short distance of Lake Garda. The yacht was probably hauled the last few miles overland. In the poem, it is described as 'dedicated to quiet age', as though it were drawn up out of the water under the terrace of Catullus's villa, a memento to his eastern travels. There is no harm, however, in supposing that he still used it for sailing on the lake and entertaining the friends who visited him from Verona, or perhaps from Rome. Since poem 11 appears to contain a reference to Caesar's expeditions to Britain, it has been placed as late as 55 or 54 B.C. This would mean that he resumed his relationship with Lesbia after his return from Bithynia. The poem is often referred to as the last poem he addressed to her. But there is little direct evidence to support this. There is nothing to indicate that it comes after poems 107 or 109. Poem 10, one of his gayest and most light-hearted pieces of *boulevarderie*, also dates from this period. In short, the tradition that he died of what our grandmothers called 'a broken heart' finds no support in the poems. It is based solely on the assumption that his love for Clodia was of the conventional type of romantic – i.e. 'fatal' – passion. But I believe that many of the poems point to an altogether different and more complicated state of mind. All we can say for certain about his death is, that like his birth, it happened. He walks out of history, off the Roman scene, and in a very short while his book – or, more likely, his books – follow him, to be lost, to all effective purpose, for a thousand years. This, or something very like it, is the most we can say we know with reasonable certitude. The rest is conjecture, more or less plausible, and more or less harmful.

The conjecture starts, and, for the most part ends, with the dating of the poems from internal evidence. This provides a framework for an inferential web of motives and personal relations. Something like a biography in embryo begins to take shape. But poetry is not like history, and for a poet to say he has done this, or felt that, is about as unsure an indication as one would wish to have that he has in fact done the one or felt the other. Besides which, studies such as these are all too often used as a substitute for poetic understanding, rather than as an aid to it; and this is especially true of the Classics. Of course, any relic of a past civilisation has an extrinsic interest as part of a whole which it is the scholar's perfectly legitimate business to reassemble. From this point of view, no one can be anything but grateful for the labour that has gone into uncovering the minutiae of dates, deaths, offices and the cross-currents of relationships among Catullus's circle. However, in a volume devoted to the interpretation of his poetry, such findings should not be allowed to assume too great an importance: their true position is that of footnotes for the archaeologically curious. With this caveat in mind, it is with a certain amount of caution that I proceed to fill in as much of the historical background as seems to me more or less relevant, and that will allow me to move on to the dubious, and somewhat unfashionable, ground of biographical conjecture.

It is only reasonable to assume (the phrase is the King Charles's Head of Catullan biography) that the Lesbia of

Catullus's poems was Clodia Metelli. There is plenty of circumstantial evidence to support the identification, and nothing against it but the caution of scholars. She was the wife of Q. Metellus Celer, her cousin on her mother's side, and they lived in the Clivus Victoriae on the Palatine, the oldest and most exclusive residential area in the city. Celer was an old-fashioned if, apparently, able politician. He was a supporter of Cicero and the Senatorial party and was Roman praetor in the year of Cicero's consulship, which was also the year of the Catiline rebellion. After he had lost the consulship to Cicero, Catiline planned to have him assassinated; but the conspiracy failed and he fled to Etruria, where an army of malcontents left over from the Sullan proscription (freedmen, known from their liberator as *Cornelii*) was waiting for him. Gaius Antonius, Mark Antony's uncle, who had been elected to the consulship with Cicero, was sent to face the rebels from the south, while Metellus Celer, who on relinquishing his praetorship had been appointed Governor of Cisalpine Gaul, was despatched to Picenum, a district on the north-west coast of the Adriatic, where he was to raise troops, cross the Po and prevent the rebels retreating through the Alps. Antonius, who had originally supported the conspirators, declined at the last moment to lead his forces into battle, and it was actually his second-in-command, Marcus Petreius, who defeated and slew Catiline in the midwinter of that year (63–62), at Pistoria, the modern Pistoia, near Florence. Those of Catiline's followers who fled northwards across the Po and fell into Metellus Celer's hands were dealt with summarily as traitors. Celer remained in Cisalpine Gaul through the spring, summer and possibly autumn of 62. We do not know when he returned to

Rome, but it would certainly not have been before his term of office was up. The province must, presumably, have been in a state of some unrest, with dissident elements using it as an escape route from the south. There is, of course, no proof that he visited, or even knew, Catullus's father; but the circle of influential or otherwise important people in a provincial capital is necessarily small. He had been of use to Caesar. (It is difficult to imagine Caesar using his house unless he was.) And he could presumably be of similar service to the new Provincial Governor, who would certainly need help and advice from local dignitaries. If Catullus had not yet left for Rome this could well have been the source of his introduction to the circle of writers, lawyers, politicians and well-bred opportunists who surrounded Metellus Celer's wife. It is almost certain* that Catullus's liaison with Clodia began before her husband's death; and that was not far ahead. At whatever date the Governor left the province, he must have been in Rome well before his election as consul in 60 B.C. By the spring of 59 he was dead.

The cause of his death is unknown; but it was common talk that he had been poisoned by Clodia herself – as it was that she had committed incest with her brother, Publius Clodius, who had a house near hers on the Palatine. It would appear that, during her husband's absence as Provincial Governor, Clodia's behaviour had become something more than a private scandal. Our source is Cicero's *Pro Caelio*. It is the only full-length picture of her, apart from what we are able to piece together from Catullus's poems; and it is a vicious onslaught. Publius Clodius had

* *Vide* poem 83 and, if the unnamed 'bright-shining goddess' refers to Clodia, 68.

accused Marcus Caelius of being involved in the Catiline conspiracy and having seduced his sister. Cicero and Clodius were bitter enemies. The more violent of Caesar's faction felt that Cicero had betrayed them by going over to the Senatorial cause on his accession to the consulship. The charge was in fact true. But on top of this, Marcus Caelius was by way of being one of Cicero's more favoured pupils in the law courts. He had certainly been accepted – and later rejected – by Clodia as a lover; but to suggest that her honour had been impugned, and that restitution was therefore necessary, was ridiculous. Both the charge itself, and the ready defence by Cicero, were undoubtedly the result of the personal antagonism between the two men. The round went to Cicero. Marcus Caelius was acquitted, and the speech securing his acquittal was one of the most skilful and impassioned that Cicero ever made. Whether it gives a true, or even a just, picture of Clodia, is another matter. I do not believe that it does.

Cicero also lived in the Clivus Victoriae. The brilliant salons that one imagines Clodia to have held for the more attractive and interesting members of the popular party took place a few doors from his house. He did not have to rely on gossip to know the sort of power she was capable of wielding, or the influence she could exert. He knew, as a former colleague, the men who surrounded her. And the way he chose to destroy her was to make her appear ridiculous. This is something that Catullus, even in his fiercest moments, never does. Perhaps from Cicero's point of view she *was* ridiculous. He was certainly ill-equipped, temperamentally and as a man, to understand a woman of her sort. But more than this, she and her circle stood for a loosening of certain of the old values and, implicitly, a readjustment of woman's place in society. The ideal of the Greek *hetæra* was alien to Rome, and not one that Cicero could be expected to welcome. He had staked his career on the survival of the old ways and the predominance of the old aristocracy. To such a person, Clodia – or her example – might well have appeared less ridiculous than dangerous; and this would have been an added inducement to Cicero to take up the case. Whether or not he succeeded in destroying her, he certainly seems to have silenced her, for it is curious that after the trial she is to all intents and purposes never heard of again. She may have remarried and become a respectable Roman matron; she may have taken up permanent residence on a country estate. She may simply have died. Her exit is as enigmatic as Catullus's.

There is a theory that poem 49, in which Catullus thanks Cicero for some unspecified favour, refers to the *Pro Caelio* speech. It is possible, but, if true, was a short-sighted reaction on Catullus's part. Cicero's Clodia leaves us with little sympathy for anyone who should be so foolish – or tasteless – as to fall in love with her. The Clodia of the poems, taking the cycle as a whole, is worth the worst she can do to a man. Catullus may wish his experience at an end; he never regrets having had it. When Cicero speaks of Clodia he does so as a judge in the divorce courts faced with a particularly 'distasteful' case. There are few things men would sooner listen to than accounts of the scandalous behaviour of noble women, provided they themselves can remain at an unembarrassing distance and are thus free to express the moral judgements of their mood. It would be pleasant to think that our forefathers were more culpable in this respect than we are. At any rate, Cicero's words have proved as potent as Catullus's, and the disdain of his *Pro*

Caelio speech finds its echo in Noel's eighteenth-century French, but tinctured with the permissive smile of the voyeur.

'*Libre alors, elle donna, sans pudeur, carrière à tous ses goûts, et porta le mépris du blâme public, jusqu'à louer un jardin sur les rives du Tibre, pour choisir parmi les baigneurs ceux qui promettraient le plus à sa fougue érotique.*'

Whatever her real nature, this was the woman who had more effect on Catullus's life than perhaps anyone else. Nor is it necessary to admit to a conventionally 'romantic' relationship to recognise that he speaks to her in an altogether different and more disturbing tone from that in which he addresses the other women in his poems. When I come to discuss the *Attis* (poem 63), I shall try to show that it was precisely her forceful and sexually dominating character that attracted him. Which was exactly what repelled Cicero.

Finally, the question has to be faced whether she did in fact become a public prostitute. That Cicero should have said she behaved like one need mean little more than that, like the divorce court judge, he disapproved of her morals. Nor, except for two poems, would there be any need to take Catullus's own words very seriously. The forms which a man's feelings of self-disgust take when a woman's demands outstrip his abilities are familiar to most of us. But poems 37 and 58 do not readily lend themselves to such an interpretation. They are too specific.

The answer, I believe, lies in the peculiar and not uncommon vice of the well-born, the rich and the secure: the desire for low-life, poverty and insecurity. Poem 58 seems to me perfectly explicable on the assumption that

Clodia was the victim of *nostalgie de la boue*. She would not be the first well-brought-up young, or not so young, woman who has gone and stood on the street corners for kicks, not quite knowing herself how serious she was. But there is more to the poem than that. The 'cross-roads and back-alleys' of line 4 sound considerably less attractive than the elegance of Tiber-fringed gardens. The tradition being that she declined from the one to the other – a lesson to us all. But 'scions of Remus', which is the literal meaning of '*Remi nepotes*', is significant. It doesn't really read as though she took on all-comers. And '*glubit*' is odd, meaning to rub the husk off an ear of corn, and hence to masturbate. It does not imply full sexual relations, and it is not difficult to imagine the sort of squalid, and basically imitative, charade that she and some of her male friends may have indulged in. Perhaps the most striking thing in the whole poem is the violent juxtaposition of the words '*glubit*' and '*magnanimi*' in the last line. The effect is as though one should say in English that a man was 'pissed under the stars'. It is a fine rhetorical device, and one that I was not able fully to capture in my translation. Instead, I tried for an additional effect of my own, which was to broaden the implied irony by retaining the actual word 'magnanimous', though with its different meaning in English. The interesting point is that the depth of feeling in the poem comes in the first three lines, with their repetitions and shifting caesurae. Not at the end where one might expect it. The comparable lines in poem 11 (17–20) strike a much harsher and more despairing note. Beside them, '*glubit magnanimi Remi nepotes*' is like a rocket exploding.

There remains the evidence of poem 37. According to a

plain reading of the text, Clodia was to be found in a tavern described as 'salacious' and frequented by the riff-raff of the town, who went there to enjoy her favours. The tavern in question is said to be 'nine pillars from the Temple of the Dioscuri'. The word used for 'pillar' is '*pila*', which refers specifically to a small pillar supporting a shop or booth. *Columna* served for the grander, more ornamental affair. Thus Catullus seems to have been indicating that one should count the number of brothels, or low drinking-dens, from the Temple of the Dioscuri. (This is a distinction that I have not been able to make clear in my version.) When I read the poem at first, I thought that this was all that I needed to know, and that I understood Catullus's directions. For the rest, I was prepared to take the poem in the same general sense as 58. But when I came to translate it I realised that there was a puzzle in the expression, 'from the Temple of the Dioscuri'. Why the Dioscuri? It told one nothing, for there was no indication in which direction one was to proceed. One could cross the Forum, in one corner of which the Temple stood. Or go down the Via Nova, beside it; or the Vicus Tuscus, behind it. It was not until one day when I was hunting for odds and ends of information about ancient Rome and turning the pages of Carnevale's *Roma Nel IIIe Secolo Dell'era Volgare* (1896), a remarkably thorough survey of the Roman antiquities then known, that I saw what I should have seen from the beginning, that the mention of the Temple of the Dioscuri was a direct reference to Publius Clodius who, as is well known, used it as a centre from which to deliver his harangues and to create public disorders. The direction now read, 'so many disreputable houses from the favourite stamping ground of Clodius and his henchmen, you will

find another disreputable house, where Clodia ... etc.'.
Evidently, either Clodia's or Clodius's own house is intended. There is no means of knowing which. A reference
to a map of ancient Rome will show that the Clivus
Victoriae runs from the Via Nova up the Palatine, beginning almost opposite the Temple of the Dioscuri. We
are no longer required to believe that Clodia lived in a
brothel.

If I seem to have laboured this point it is because I believe
that the solution that I have offered is less inherently unlikely than that a woman of her background and, from
what we can understand of the poems, of her sexual tem-
perament, became in reality and earnest a prostitute. The
question will always remain open, and to an extent hinges
on what we understand by the word 'prostitute'. After all,
for Cicero a *hetæra* was a prostitute, and in his opinion
Clodia had stooped to become a form of *hetæra*. For
Catullus, if she slept with another man, she was a prostitute.
It may be asked, what chance did the woman have?

The date of Catullus's introduction into Roman society
is of interest in helping to assess how much of his younger,
formative life was spent in what he refers to as 'the province'. It is, unfortunately, likely to remain an unsolved
query. If Metellus Celer was responsible, Catullus would
not be likely to have left home before the spring of 62.
On the other hand, his father, who must have been a
wealthy man, was probably just as capable of arranging the
matter for himself. In which case, there is no knowing
when he left. There is a third alternative – of no help from
the point of view of dates, but worth considering for other
reasons. It is not impossible that he was provided with
introductions to Roman literary circles by Publius Valerius

Cato, the Veronese teacher, poet and critic, known not only to Catullus but to at least three other of the 'new poets', Ticidas, Gaius Cinna and Furius Bibaculus, all Cisalpines and all, at one time or another, pupils of his. It is likely, but unprovable, that Catullus was another. Cato was the author of a work on grammar, now lost, and probably of a poem called *Dirae*, which is still extant. A line of Cinna's refers to a poem called *Diana*, and a line of Ticidas', although not quite so certainly, to one called *Lydia*. Bibaculus speaks of him as though he were not only a master but an exemplar. He calls him 'the sole maker of poets', and laments the poverty of so discerning an individual. The warmth and personal element in Bibaculus's tributes, together with Catullus's poem (56), give us a hint of the mingled feelings of equality and respect which these men seem to have felt for him. If, as most scholars believe, Cato was the moving force behind the 'new poets', it would help to explain the number of Cisalpines among them. It would also explain, perhaps, something of the urgency and iconoclasm – although that word may be too strong – that they brought to their work. It would be misleading to suggest that, because they came from across the Po, an area which had not yet acquired full Roman status, they were what we should call 'provincials'. But there would be a freshness about them, and this – as in the case of Catullus – would give a bite to their Roman manners. Cato himself outlived all his pupils, dying as late as 25 B.C., only eight or nine years before Propertius, whose work, if he read it, he must certainly have approved of.

When we speak of the 'new poets' and the inspiration they derived from Cato, it should be remembered that we are in effect speaking of the work of Catullus and a tradition about Cato. The surviving fragments of the works of Calvus, Cinna, Cornificius, Bibaculus and Ticidas occupy barely three pages of print. Fortunately, in at least ten of his poems Catullus gives some very direct indications of what he and his friends felt about poetry, what their prejudices were and what they expected from it. Most of these poems are written to fellow poets and cast in the form of imaginary letters. (Catullus was fond of this convention: the opening lines of poem 13 follow the actual wording of a formal invitation to dinner.) Some of these 'letters' promise, or enclose, or make excuses for not enclosing translations of Greek models. Others are humorously abusive of poets of whom Catullus disapproves. Others are tributes to friends. We gather that the followers of the old-fashioned tradition of Roman epic were not popular with the 'new poets'; that long-windedness was to be avoided, and anything pompous, stilted or affected. We are told, or it is implied, that gaiety should be a concomitant of the arts, that the psychological and personal approach was to be preferred to the formal or public one, and that elegance (*venustas*), taste and learning (*doctrina*), were among a poet's most precious jewels. Perhaps the most illuminating poem of this genre is No. 50, where we see Calvus and Catullus, like any two poets who are also friends, playing at poetry together. We are aware that their poetry was a very close part of their lives. This was something new in Roman letters.

There is always the danger that the literary historian will invest the past with a more or less spurious unity. Life, we feel, is more haphazard than most biographers or historians would like it to appear. The documentary evidence for the idea that there was a new movement at all rests on three

brief passages of Cicero, in one of which appears the term
'new poets' – and, as an ironic allusion to their literary
ancestry, 'new poets' is written in Greek. To some people
this has seemed insufficient proof of the existence of a
literary movement, and they have consequently denied
that the so-called 'new poets' worked together or formed
a school. And yet one of the strongest impressions left from
a reading of the dozen or so poems mentioned above is that
Catullus, and the other writers with whom he mixed, felt
themselves united, in an almost arrogant manner, *for* certain things in poetry, and *against* others, and this seems to
me stronger evidence than Cicero's.

When Catullus started writing in 69 or 68 B.C. he had
three traditions to draw on: Roman epic and tragedy;
Roman comedy and satire; and the Roman love epigram,
which was an importation from Alexandrian Greek. This
third element was comparatively new, with a history of not
more than fifty years. The examples we have are elegant
but brittle; slight in accomplishment and small in quantity.
The weightier traditions of tragedy and epic were not without Greek influence; but beside them the love epigram is
like an exotic that had not taken root. By setting out these
trends, in this way, I do not wish to imply that they were of
equal importance, either in themselves or to Catullus. They
were not. The exact nature of his debt to each is a matter of
dispute. In general terms, however, it is safe to say that he
drew his ability to convey grandeur (the Aegeus passage
in poem 64) from the language of epic and tragedy; that he
guessed at the uses to which colloquialism and realism
might be put from the comico-satiric tradition; and that it
was in the last, the somewhat precious form of the love
epigram, that he saw the opportunity for original develop-

ment. But a poet's greatness rests largely on the extent to which he is able to effect a synthesis of preceding traditions while producing something that has not been achieved before. This provides the fourth element: the constant and individual interplay between the three traditions. Fused in the *œuvre*, it is what gives Catullus's poetry its immediacy and, as far as Latin literature is concerned, its originality. Before Catullus, colloquialism had been confined to comedy; the elevated manner to epic or tragedy. In his poetry, for the first time, grandeur is heightened by unexpected realism. Colloquial diminutives express tenderness, which rubs shoulders with an equally colloquial grossness. The subject matter of the Roman epigram is broadened and shifted to the entirely new field of the personal lyric with a wide variety of metres, many of which are used for the first time. As for his own epigrams, he confined these, for the most part, to elegiacs and, in so doing, made the brittleness of the epigrammatic technique, once a limitation of the poetic sensibility, an end in itself, so that his most vitriolic fantasies become disembodied and intellectualised: imagery and metaphor are discarded and a startling directness of language takes their place. But the most important thing Catullus does for the Alexandrian Greek epigram is to make it personal.

The Greek stimulus sought by the 'new poets' came mainly from Alexandria. The reason for this was natural enough. Ever since its foundation by Alexander in 332 B. C., and the subsequent building of the great library by Ptolemy I (323–283), it had been the principal centre of Greek culture and learning. It represented what Greece meant to a contemporary. It would be unrealistic to expect writers to have gone behind Alexandria to Greece itself. Her judgements (in literary matters) were regarded as the judgements of Greece, or the Greek cities. Added to this, Alexandria had, in the second century B.C., come under Rome's sphere of influence, and as recently as the year 80 had actually been bequeathed to Rome by Ptolemy X in his will. The focal point for the scholars and poets of Alexandria was, of course, the magnificent library, the greatest in the world, carefully nursed, for their own political ends, by the Ptolemies. Callimachus himself, whom the 'new poets' seem to have held in especial regard, worked and taught there from c. 260 B.C. to his death in 250. Apollonius Rhodius (c. 295–c. 230), whose *Argonautica*, so sympathetic to modern tastes, was clearly known to Catullus, was a pupil of his. This was where the 'new poets' derived their ideal of the scholar-poet. It was here that they learnt to attach as much importance to the complexity of a poet's attitudes as to their consistency; it was here that they learnt their love of allusion and the oblique manner, and to cultivate an almost eighteenth-century type of artistic sensibility. It was here they learnt their respect for craftsmanship and their devotion to form and structure. But the 'new poets' applied these Alexandrian principles and techniques to a very un-Alexandrian situation. The Alexandrian school had been engaged in resuscitating, and to some degree had succeeded in embalming, an old tradition; the 'new poets' were endeavouring to found a new one. When considering the Alexandrian school as a whole, it is permissible to regret the lack of (apparent) spontaneity which characterised the earlier age of the Greek lyric. But spontaneity, or its appearance, is by no means the *sine qua non* of a successful poem. We regret its absence only in certain moods. To compare a poem of T. S. Eliot's to 'Go

Lovely Rose' and find Eliot wanting, is to indulge in an extra-literary judgement. Only a prejudice against Alexandrianism, as such, could lead us to deplore its deep and widespread influence over Catullus and his circle. They – or Catullus – had plenty of 'spontaneity', and if his more substantial works, such as poems 64 and 68, do at times read a little like *The Waste Land*, they seem none the worse for that.

The longer works (61–8) stand in the middle of the volume of his poems as it has come down to us, and deserve special mention. But first there is the volume itself, which is curiously arranged. It is in three parts: mixed lyrics, long poems and epigrams. The epigrams are nearly all quite short. Poem 76, the longest, runs to no more than twenty-six lines, and may more properly be called a love elegy. With 68, it represents the first example of its kind in Latin. This section is introduced, metrically, by the second half of the long poems, 65–8, which are all in elegiacs. The lyrics (1–60) are in various metres, sapphics, choliambics, iambic trimeters, and the metre which Catullus made peculiarly his own, the Phalaecian hendecasyllable, which appears to be calculatedly inserted between the others. Poem 34, the hymn to Diana, is the only one in this group to be written in glyconics, and, as with the elegiacs and poems 65–8, so here we find that the *first* of the long poems is also written in glyconics. It is clear that whoever arranged the poems did so on an almost exclusively metrical basis. This would suggest that the arrangement was at least post-Augustan. But the decisive factor is the length of the whole book – approximately 2,300 lines. This was enough to fill nearly three rolls; and the roll did not give place to our book form until the third or fourth century A.D. A likely theory is that poems 1–60 were originally a collection on their own, perhaps arranged by Catullus and preceded by the dedication to Cornelius Nepos. Various of the long poems, notably 64, would have been published as individual items, while the poems at the end may only have been passed round privately among intimates. There is no means of knowing whether they are complete, or whether they are a selection. While they contain some of Catullus's best and most characteristic work, they are of varying worth, and are certainly more scrappily arranged than the lyrics.

Turning to the long poems, we see that 61 is in the form of a personal epithalamium. Its recipient was Lucius Manlius Torquatus, a close friend of Catullus; about the wife we know nothing. Poem 62 is another epithalamium, but generalised. Taken with poem 34, it is one of the only two non-personal or public poems that he ever wrote. It is written in hexameters. Poem 63 is the celebrated *Attis*. The subject is again the relationship between male and female, but it is treated psychologically, in terms of Catullus's own experience, which he projects into the world of myth. It is written in the galliambic metre, so-called from the priests of Cybele, the *galli*, from whose ritual cries and dance movements it was said to be derived. It is the only poem to have survived in this metre either in Latin or Greek. Poem 64 blends each of the foregoing elements: it is mythological; love is a public, official affair (the marriage of Peleus and Thetis), and a private one (Ariadne's elopement, desertion and consolation). Like 62 it is in hexameters; they are the only two poems he wrote in this metre, and it will be seen that they neatly sandwich the unique galliambics. Poem 65 introduces three new subjects: poetry itself, friendship and the loss of his brother. It is a dedicatory epistle to 66 and is addressed to Q. Hortensius Hortalus. It initiates the series written in elegiacs. Poem 66 itself is a direct translation from a poem of Callimachus', an elegant piece of court poetry verging on persiflage. Nothing – or little – is accidental in Catullus, least of all the subject matter of a translated poem. (Poem 51, his other direct translation, is further proof of this.) In No. 66 he chose a poem in which the protagonist – a woman's lock of hair – laments the fact that it was severed from its mistress's head on her wedding night, before she had had time to experience the pleasures of married love. The lock recounts the occasion and its circumstances, concluding with a request for votive offerings of the scents used by married women,* since it never experienced these in life. If wives preface the 'chaste dalliance of the marriage bed' with libations such as these, they will be blest with arts which will keep their husbands faithful to them. I believe that Catullus has exaggerated the element of persiflage that he found in the original and used his subject matter as an opportunity to turn the poem he is translating inside out and thus make a personal poem out of a quasi official one. (Callimachus wrote the piece very soon after the events which it describes.) Poem 67, set in 'the province', consists of a dialogue between Catullus and the door of an unnamed woman. The Caecilius who is spoken of as having right of access to the house may be the fellow poet of No. 35, who had written a poem, presumably not unlike the *Peleus and Thetis*, on Cybele. Unfortunately, the local allusions are lost on us. We are confronted with (at the least) incest and adultery, and an attempt to swindle an inheritance out of someone under the Lex Voconia, whereby a daughter was unable to inherit

* Married and unmarried women used different scents, just as they wore their hair differently.

a substantial sum unless she produced a male child, in which case she could hold the money in trust. (The same reference is found in Poem 68.) The poem is amusing, coarse, realistic, and presents us with the obverse of 61 and 62. Poem 68 is addressed to Manlius Torquatus. I accept the theory that Manlius's wife, Aurunculeia, has died, and that the poem is principally one of consolation. But Manlius's love and loss is intricately interwoven with Catullus's own loss (of his brother) and love (of Lesbia). The themes of friendship and poetry make their reappearance. If 67 was local and realistic, 68 is local and romantic. Mythology is used again, but not now as a framework, as in 64. In 64 the mythological landscape was touched with realistic detail. Here, the world of reality is irradiated by myth. The poem has a trancelike quality.

Enough should have been said to show that this middle section contains poems that are essential to an understanding of Catullus, and that cannot be regarded separately from the rest of his work. If this seems a curious statement to the reader who has read my translations but is no Catullan scholar, then one of the purposes of my version will have been achieved. Not only do these poems form a unity in themselves but in their unreal and, in the *Attis*, violent and catastrophic, handling of the sexual relationship, they cast backwards to the extremes of tenderness, in the lyrics, and forwards to the obscenities of the Gellius sequence. (There are 'obscene' poems in section 1–60, and warm and tender poems in section 69–116; but as a generalization the distinction may be allowed to stand.) Catullus is, of course, a lyric poet. But, as far as the middle section is concerned 61 is nothing if not lyric; 65 and 68 both have very great lyrical beauty of a grave and meditative kind; while no man should imagine he can fully apprehend the spirit which in-forms the sparrow or the kissing poems, unless he has the *Attis* in his other hand. The objection to the longer poems would seem to resolve itself into an objection to 64. Since 64, together with 68, were doubtless the poems which he himself regarded most highly, another look at both of them would seem to be indicated.

Poem 64 is the centrepiece of the *Carmina*. It is a window on the world of the gods. If to-day we look back over our shoulders a thousand years or so we do not, even if we are G. K. Chesterton Distributists, feel that we have missed-out on Eden. But a similar idea does appear to have haunted both Greeks and Romans round about the beginning of the Christian era. It was no mere accident of literary fancy that insisted that all genealogies, whether of city, state or hero, should be traced back to the time when the gods still walked the earth. This feeling was the inspiration of the Evander passages in the *Aeneid*, of the whole of Ovid's sprawling *Metamorphoses* and, of course, of the *Peleus and Thetis*. Although the part played by Crete in the early history of the Aegean basin was then unknown, it is plain from both myth and legend that the Minoan age was in some obscure way recognised as the time when this de-sirable state obtained. In the *Peleus and Thetis* Catullus employs all the resources of a highly eclectic and allusive use of myth to depict its passing. In a sense, his method allows him to have things both ways. He can pin-point details which serve his purpose, but even while he is doing this the body of the material he does *not* use still exerts its influence over the reader's mind. Taking the Argonautic expedition as a whole, the fact that Peleus leant over the side of the ship and saw and fell in love with the sea-nymph

Thetis, is of such slight importance that it might well pass unmentioned; while Ariadne, deserted on Naxos, and Aegeus, committing suicide because of the wrong coloured sail, are traditionally, and rightly, regarded as postscripts to the Minotaur myth. Yet it is from the interlocking of details such as these, taken from quite separate mythological cycles, that Catullus conjures his orderly, consistent and convincing narrative. His points of departure are pre-Homeric Crete, the marriage of Peleus and Thetis, and Troy. The connection between them is effected (backwards to Crete) by the wedding quilt, and (forwards to Troy) by the ill-omened epithalamium. We are shown how the fall of Minoan Crete marked a process which, via the birth of Achilles, found its conclusion in the fall of Troy. As though this were not enough, Catullus also manages to tell us what the golden age once meant in terms of human happiness and what the future held in terms of human distress. He describes how a goddess marries a man, and a woman marries a god. A life of heroic action is rewarded in the first instance, and love is eased of its passion in the second. (Ariadne, as a victim of faithlessness and unrequited love, is a mouthpiece for Catullus's own feelings.) He also shows Nemesis overtaking evil (Aegeus's suicide), a foretaste of the state into which the world is about to lapse. The way in which the whole poem folds inwards on itself to the seventy lines of Ariadne's lament, which represents the 'personal' centre of the poem, is perhaps best shown in tabulated form.

ll. 1–49: The Argonautic expedition on which Peleus first sees Thetis; the wedding day; the Palace; the coverlet on the marriage bed.

ll. 50–264: Description of the scenes woven on the coverlet. This section is divisible as follows:

ll. 50–75: Ariadne on the beach at Naxos; the intrusion
of evil in the shape of human faithlessness;

ll. 76–123: flashback of Theseus' expedition to Crete, the
slaying of the Minotaur and Theseus' subsequent
elopement with Ariadne;

ll. 124–31: return to Ariadne on Naxos;

ll. 132–201: Ariadne's lament and curse;

ll. 202–14: the Gods, as Theseus nears Greece, hear
Ariadne's curse;

ll. 215–37: flashback of Aegeus's instructions to Theseus
before he set sail for Crete, and Aegeus's feelings on
that occasion;

ll. 238–48: return to the present; Theseus forgets his instructions; Aegeus commits suicide; Theseus' state of
mind is compared to

ll. 249–50: that of Ariadne as she stands gazing out to
sea after him;

ll. 251–64: the scene passes forward to the advent of
Bacchus which ends the description of the coverlet.

ll. 265–77: Departure of the mortal guests.

ll. 278–304: Advent of the immortals – the Olympians,
Jupiter and Juno, attended by the three demi-gods particularly associated with the bride and bridegroom.
First: Chiron, the local deity of the chief mountain of
Thessaly, Pelion, and the future tutor of Achilles;
secondly, Peneus, spirit of the principal river and related
to Thetis; and thirdly, Prometheus, who foreseeing the
glory that will accrue from the marriage has persuaded
Jupiter to sanction it. Apollo, who is to be the author of

Achilles' death, is mentioned as staying behind on Olympus.

ll. 305–22: Description of the Parcae.

ll. 323–81: Hymn of the Parcae, constituting the epithalamium; the scene moves forward as the Fates foretell the birth of Achilles and the subsequent fall of Troy.

ll. 382–408: Final peroration on the fallen state of man and the vanished golden age with which the poem has opened.

The total effect is cinematic. We have glimpses of paradisal landscapes emerging from the clear, primal world of sea and sky. But the clarity is deceptive and the landscapes and figures dissolve into one another and are never fully revealed. All is a little mysterious; which is as it should be; for without mystery there is no paradise.

The second of Catullus's Alexandrian pieces (68) is even more complex. Unfortunately, the text is very corrupt. We do not even know for certain whether it is one poem or two. (In the original codex, now lost, there was no indication where one poem ended and another began, and the copyist, after a break in his work, was quite capable of taking up his pen again at the wrong place.) It is unlikely that the string of queries which the poem prompts will ever be satisfactorily resolved. If it *is* one poem, is it addressed to 'Allius', or 'Mallius', and is this person identifiable with L. Manlius Torquatus of poem 61? Is the *domina* of the house which has been lent to Catullus for his meetings with Lesbia(?) its *châtelaine*, or Torquatus's mistress or both? And is his wife, Aurunculeia, dead? And is her death really the main subject of the poem or, more accurately, the core around which the poem is built? As elsewhere, I have taken different readings from different texts, and different suggestions from different scholars – usually I have found that it has been the more traditional interpretation that has attracted me – and having selected my material on the basis of what I found most stimulating poetically, I have then tried to rewrite the poem as I imagined Catullus might have written it had he been alive to-day and writing in English. As a poem is more than the sum of its constituent parts, a certain ruthlessness over details is often necessary. It is the whole poem which has to be captured and rewritten. One is, of course, grateful for whatever *donnés* fall into one's lap, *passim*. But the details of a poem are to be digested so that they become a part of the living grain of the new poem, not embalmed like flies in ointment. Since 68 is not a narrative poem, a table setting out the various strands of which it is composed will need to be a little more explanatory than was the case with 64.

ll. 1–40: Preface. Manlius has written to Catullus asking him for 'gifts of Love and the Muses' to console him in his sorrow. Catullus replies by saying that his own sorrows match Manlius's, and that he cannot comfort him as he would wish. Manlius's sorrow consists of the loss of his young wife, Aurunculeia; Catullus's of the loss of his brother.

ll. 41–73: Catullus nevertheless decides to record the debt that he owes to Manlius, who once provided him with a house in which he could meet Lesbia and in which they could make love. She comes to him as a 'bright-shining goddess'.

ll. 74–86: His own love for Lesbia, and the dead Aurunculeia's for Manlius are fused in the image of Laodamia, the symbol of wifely passion. (See Glossary.)

ll. 87–90: Troy, where Laodamia lost her husband, Protesilaus, is apostrophised in the first of two bridge passages as a source of widespread sorrow. (There may be a connection here with the 'historical' view of Troy expressed in 64, where its fall marks the end of the golden age.) Through Troy, Laodamia's loss is linked to Catullus's and so to Manlius's. In the intensity of her love she represents Aurunculeia, and of her grief, Manlius.

ll. 91–100: Catullus's brother was buried near Troy. The theme of his dead brother was broached in the first section of the poem; it is taken up again and expanded. Catullus repeats the original lines (20–4) nearly word for word.

ll. 101–4: The second of the bridge passages about the Trojan War. It is worth noting that Helen is mentioned by name in the first, and Paris in the second. In themselves the two passages constitute a laconic reflection – from outside the body of the poem – on the inherently calamitous nature of mortal love.

ll. 105–30: Catullus passes from the cause of Laodamia's grief to an analysis of her love. He does this by means of three sustained similes, each to do with a different sort of bird: the Stymphalian birds of Hercules's Sixth Labour, the vulture, and mating doves. The poetic significance of the passage has puzzled commentators. Catullus's technique is similar to that of our seventeenth-century Metaphysicals. In lines 74–86, Laodamia's love is evoked in such a way that we are intended to participate in it; here the intention is that we should understand it. The passages complement each other.

To take the similes in order: I read the caverns under Mount Cyllene as a reference to the consummation of the marriage. Hercules can stand only for Manlius. We cannot know what his Sixth Labour suggested to a man of Catullus's day: but there can be no doubt that in the context of the poem the derivation of the word 'Stymphalus' (φαλλός and στύμα: the male and female members) is of peculiar significance. The reference to Hebe, goddess of eternal youth, whom Hercules marries on his apotheosis, indicates that Aurunculeia, still young, will be reunited with Manlius in the next world. In the second simile, the vulture symbolises death. The woman's gifts that the bride (Laodamia) brings will keep even death at bay. In the third simile, Isis's vulture gives place to Venus's doves which symbolise the enjoyment of sexual love. In brief, we have (a) ritualistic loss of virginity; (b) the expectations and the transforming power of love; (c) sexual pleasure.

ll. 131–48: Reintroduction of the theme of Catullus and Lesbia's love for each other. Their illicit relationship is compared with that of married love.

ll. 149–60: Epilogue. Catullus has, after all, written a poem to Manlius. Not a formal piece, such as he sent to Hortalus in 66, but an account of their relations with each other. The poem ends with a final evocation of Lesbia as 'she who endows Catullus with the quality of vision'.

I have often felt that the poem reads like an expansion of 65. Both poems consist of a similar, elaborate interweaving of the themes on which Catullus felt most deeply. Both have the same slow-trailing movement of successive clauses loosely drawn out. But what made the poem new in Latin, and remains its outstanding virtue, is the calculated and delicate use of myth to delineate specific psychological states. It is a reminder of what we may well have lost in the works of Calvus, Cinna and the other 'new poets'.

There remains the *Attis*. Walter Savage Landor's comment with which he concludes his long survey of Doering's second edition of the *Carmina* (published nearly fifty years after his first, Leipzig, 1788) provides a fitting and amusing prelude to any discussion of the poem.

They who have listened, patiently and supinely, to the catarrhal songsters of goose-grazed commons, will be loth and ill-fitted to mount up with Catullus to the highest steeps in the forests of Ida, and will shudder at the music of the Corybantes in the temple of the Great Mother of the Gods.

The poem is a strange one, both violent and barbaric, full of odd coinings and archaisms, and written in the breakneck metre known as 'galliambic'. The youth Attis is described as crossing the sea to Asia Minor and there castrating himself in the frenzy of his devotion to the Mother Goddess. The act is accompanied in the original Latin by a change of gender. Attis calls to the other initiates of Cybele's cult to join him at her shrine on Mount Ida. There he falls into a coma. On waking, his immediate reaction is to regret what he has done. He returns to the beach and looks back over the sea. There follows a twenty-three-line lament for the civilised patrimony which he has abandoned. This patrimony is described in Greek terms, not Roman, a fact which has led some scholars to presume a Greek model, even a Greek original, and to read the whole as an expression of conflict between civilised and barbaric values. Even if such an interpretation is correct, it still leaves the core of the poem untouched. Following Attis's lament, Cybele unyokes one of her lions and instructs it to drive Attis back into the thickets on the slopes of Ida, where he is to remain for the rest of his life, a helpless devotee. In the last three lines, Catullus prays to Cybele to protect him from such desires; 'goad others to rabid madness; keep your fury from my house'. The lines are spoken as though he has woken from a nightmare (the preceding ninety lines) and recognised, with horror, himself in the figure of the unfortunate Attis. To emphasise this reading I have placed the last four lines of my version in direct quotes.

When considering the significance of this poem, I have always found it suggestive that the Temple of Cybele stood not far from Clodia's house, on the Palatine. The clashing cymbals, the drums and the peculiar ululating cries of the worshippers must on occasion have been audible to the members of Metellus Celer's household. Whether the initial stimulus that Catullus found in the myth lay simply in an accident of locality such as this, or whether it was the result of his trip to Asia Minor, it is impossible to say. The worship of Cybele had been introduced into Rome in the year 204 B.C., during the Second Punic War. A black stone representing the Goddess had been brought up the Tiber and placed, temporarily, in the Temple of Victoria, since the new temple which was designed to house it had not yet been completed. The cult was of Anatolian origin and was ecstatic like that of Dionysus, some of the terms being interchangeable. The general effect of both has been described as not unlike a latter-day Dervish dance. The worshippers inflicted wounds on themselves, were liable to despatch anyone who stumbled on their devotions, and, in the rites of the Mother Goddess, actually underwent voluntary castration. The fundamentally grave Romans viewed the cult with suspicion, and it was not allowed to spread.

On many occasions, in moments of intense emotion, Catullus expresses his feelings in the guise of a woman. The fact that homosexuality was not then considered either as a vice, an aberration or a disease, as it is now, is attendant but not cardinal to the point that I wish to make, which is that there was in Catullus a strain of femininity which went deeper than 'normal' adherence to the bisexual conventions of his class and time. His Iuventius poems strike exactly the same note as the heterosexual poems such as 32, that were not written to Clodia. The absence of 'guilt' is matched by a similar absence of 'spirituality' – of anything that is not a straightforward satisfaction of desire. With Clodia, lust is at a discount. It is she, to speak from the evidence of the poems, who displays the animality, not him. In No. 72 he even compares his feelings for her with those of a father for his daughter: an attitude unique in Roman poetry. Poem 51 is a translation from Sappho. It is the poem in which he gives Clodia the name of 'Lesbia'. In it, not only does he speak to her in the person of Sappho but the poem he has chosen to translate is one in which Sappho describes the physical sensations she experiences from the close presence of her beloved, in her case, if we accept the tradition, another woman. In the beautiful, tentacular 65, the startling, bright little vignette at the end (which is in itself a brilliant switch from the inclusive to the elliptical) represents an identification of himself with a young girl who is caught harbouring a guilty secret, the secret being her awareness of her own sexuality, symbolised by an apple. In poem 2, he wishes he were able to play with

Lesbia's sparrow, *as Lesbia does*, and imagines that if he were, he would feel like Atalanta, when she stooped to pick up the apple and so lost the foot-race and, with it, her virginity. In No. 66, we have observed how he assumes the *persona* of a woman's lock of hair; while in No. 68 we noted a similar switch of sexes in the passages where he describes Manlius's and his own grief in terms of Laodamia's. But there is an obverse to this side of Catullus's nature. It is to be found in his obsession with the more repulsive aspects of sexuality. (Poem 97 and the Gellius sequence.) His male drives found their outlet here, and the more disagreeable the news they could report, the more justification they provided for his invert fantasies. In poem 11 he refers to Lesbia as 'dragging the guts' out of him in the love act; and elsewhere there are references to the way in which a woman 'drains' a man of virility. It is as though Catullus felt that at the moment of orgasm a man became like Cybele's priests behind Metellus Celer's house. This I believe to have been the significance of the Attis myth for Catullus. Woman has, as it were, a lien on man's sex, an attitude expressed in the priests' castration and in the dramatic change of gender in the poem. It is the reason why Catullus was both repelled and attracted by the myth. The hate which Attis proclaims for Venus in line 17 is identical with that which Catullus in poem 85 expresses for Clodia. It has nothing to do with the antipathy of discordant elements, but arises from the repulsion from which attraction draws its strength, each succeeding the other in the love–hate see-saw. The experience is, of course, that of the manic depressive. And the *Attis*, as is now generally accepted, is a document of that state.

As a footnote to the poem, it is worth recalling the story

of how an ancestress of Clodia's vindicated her chastity by using her *zona* or girdle, to secure the image of the Holy Mother when the ship bringing it up the Tiber ran aground in shoal water. It is unclear exactly how she did this, but the garment in question was evidently used to bring the image (it was probably a meteorite) safely to dry land. Clodia must have known the tradition. And Catullus too. Did he perceive and, if so, relish, the irony it contained for him?

As I have intimated above, I have followed no one text in my translation. The original codex, which according to a venerable tradition was discovered wedging a wine barrel in Verona, at the end of the thirteenth century A.D., was in a poor state. There were frequent *lacunae* in the text, attributable (according to the same tradition) to the operation of the wine on the parchment. Worse than this, the codex itself disappeared again as mysteriously as it had appeared, although fortunately not before at least two copies had been taken. The efforts of scholars have since then been directed towards establishing the readings of this lost codex by collating the various copies – and copies of copies – which were taken from it. R. A. B. Mynors' recension is the most recent and among the most valuable contributions in this field. Unfortunately, as with C. J. Fordyce's volume, it appeared too late for me to make full use of it. Of the three almost certainly spurious poems, I have included No. 18, but followed Professor Mynors in omitting Nos. 19 and 20. Apart from this, I have taken 2b as part of 2 and have omitted 14b; I have taken 58b as part of 55; 78b as part of 78, and 95b as part of 95.

The hills around Lake Garda can have altered little since Catullus's day, and the waters of the lake not at all. Garda

is subject to very swift changes of weather. The wind off
the Dolomites blows down over Trento to Riva at the head
of the lake. The hills which stand close in to the northern
shore conduct the wind from one end of Garda to the other.
Suddenly the water will be curled into steep, crested waves,
so that the lake looks like the open sea. A very slight shift
of wind and the waters will be smooth again. The pleasure
boats which in the tourist season ply north and south between Riva, Malcesine and Desenzano wisely hug the
coast. The violent and abrupt changes of mood which
characterise the lake are also characteristic of Catullus's
poetry. They are each as unpredictable as the other. But the
lake could be called – is invariably and justly called –
'beautiful', and that is not the aptest word to apply to
Catullus's poetry. There is immediacy and vitality and
pathos and nobility. He riddles away with words, juggling
them about, a dozen times in half as many lines: eyes,
apples, stars, numbers and then more numbers. The primi-
tive is sometimes surprisingly near the surface. He has
made his own mirror, not of life but of himself, and in this
of course he is a Romantic. The tributes to him in English
poetry are innumerable. They start with Ben Jonson, and
go through Lovelace to Landor and Tennyson, Swin-
burne, Arthur Symons, Yeats and Ezra Pound. And when
I think how I shall conclude this tribute of mine, I turn
again to Walter Savage Landor whom I have just quoted
and whose paraphrases and adaptations stand second only
to those of Ben Jonson. The lines touch on the problem of
Catullus's 'obscenity'. Landor, whom no one could accuse
of laxity in this respect, saw that the question was of little or
no importance in itself, and existed only in an incidental
relationship to the whole work. The picture is a charming

one, and not without relevance in these days of hasty and intemperate opinions on the subject of what should and should not be printed.

> '*Tell me not what too well I know*
> *About the bard of Sirmio –*
> *Yes, in Thalia's son*
> *Such stains there are – as when a Grace*
> *Sprinkles another's laughing face*
> *With nectar, and runs on.*'

St Briavels, Glos., 1944 –
Tirolo di Merano, 1965

THE POEMS

I

To whom should I present this
little book so carefully polished
but to you, Cornelius, who have always
been so tolerant of my verses,
                              you
who of us all has dared
to take the whole of human history
as his field
          – three doctoral and weighty volumes!
Accept my book, then, Cornelius
for what it's worth,
          and may the Muse herself
turn as tolerant an eye upon these songs
          in days to come.

Lesbia's sparrow!
              Lesbia's plaything!
in her lap or at her breast
when Catullus's desire
                gleams
and fancies playing at something,
                    perhaps precious,
a little solace for satiety
                when love has ebbed,
    you are invited to nip her finger
    you are coaxed into pecking sharply,
if I could play with you
               her sparrow
lifting like that my sorrow
                I should be eased
as the girl was of her virginity
when the miniature apple,
                 gold/undid
her girl's girdle
       – too long tied.

3

Who loves beauty
             veil her statues
veil Venus
       her attendant Cupids
Lesbia's plaything
            Lesbia's sparrow
                    is dead
dearer to her than her two eyes
sweeter than honey
         closer (even) than the young girl to her mother,
in her lap or at her breast
hopping from one shoulder to another
cheeping continually
              to its mistress alone

... has now hopped solitarily
down that dark alleyway of no return
evil shadows of the underworld
                Orcus
who swallows up all beautiful things
needless act! a small bird!
to close in on Lesbia's sparrow,

and swelling my girl's veiled eyes
               which redden with tears.

4

My bean-pod boat you see here
        friends & guests
will tell you
        if you ask her
that she's been
        the fastest piece of timber
under oar or sail
        afloat.
Call as witness
        the rough Dalmatian coast
the little islands of the Cyclades
Colossan Rhodes
        the savage Bosphorus
the unpredictable surface of the Pontic Sea
where
        near Cytorus
before you were a yacht
you stood
        part of some wooded slope
where the leaves speak continuously in sibilants together.
Pontic Amastris
        Cytorus
– stifled with box-wood –
        these things
my boat affirms
        are common knowledge to you both.
More:
        you witnessed the beginning
        when she stood
straight on a hill-ridge behind the port,

in your waters
>you saw the new oar-blades first flash,
thence through the impetuous seas
carrying her owner
>the call
first to lee
>then to larboard
sometimes the wind-god falling full on the blown sheet.
Finally,
>no claim on the protection of any sea god
on the long voyage up to this clear lake.

These things have all gone by.
Drawn up here
>gathering quiet age
she dedicates herself gratefully to you
the heavenly twins
>Castor & Pollux
the Dioscuri.

5

Lesbia
   live with me
& love me so
we'll laugh at all
the sour-faced strict-
ures of the wise.
This sun once set
will rise again,
when our sun sets
follows night &
an endless sleep.
Kiss me now a
thousand times &
now a hundred
more & then a
hundred & a
thousand more again
till with so many
hundred thousand
kisses you & I
shall both lose count
nor any can
from envy of
so much of kissing
put his finger
on the number
of sweet kisses
you of me &
I of you,
   darling, have had.

6

Your most recent acquisition, Flavius,
must be as unattractive as
                              (doubtless) she is unacceptable
or you would surely have told us about her.
You are wrapped up with a whore to end all whores
and ashamed to confess it.
                              You do not spend bachelor nights.
Your divan, reeking of Syrian unguents,
draped with bouquets & blossoms etc.
                              proclaims it,
the pillows & bedclothes indented in several places,
a ceaseless jolting & straining of the framework
the shaky accompaniment to your sex parade.
Without more discretion your silence is pointless.
Attenuated thighs betray your preoccupation.
Whoever, whatever she is, good or bad,
                              tell us, my friend –
Catullus will lift the two of you & your love-acts into the
    heavens
in the happiest of his hendecasyllables.

7

Curious to learn
how many kiss-
es of your lips
might satisfy
my lust for you,
Lesbia, know
as many as
are grains of sand
between the oracle
of sweltering Jove
at Ammon &
the tomb of old
Battiades the First,
in Libya
where the silphium grows;
alternatively,
as many as
the sky has stars
at night shining
in quiet upon
the furtive loves
of mortal men,
as many kiss-
es of your lips
as these might slake
your own obsessed
Catullus, dear,
so many that
no prying eye
can keep the count

nor spiteful tongue fix
their total in
a fatal formula.

8

Break off
            fallen Catullus
                        time to cut losses,
bright days shone once,
            you followed a girl
                        here & there
loved as no other
            perhaps
                        shall be loved,
then was the time
            of love's *insouciance*,
                        your lust as her will
matching.
            Bright days shone
                        on both of you.
Now,
            a woman is unwilling.
                        Follow suit
weak as you are
            no chasing of mirages
                        no fallen love,
a clean break
            hard against the past.
                        Not again, Lesbia.
No more.
            Catullus is clear.
                        He won't miss you.
He won't crave it.
            It is cold.
                        But you will whine.

[59]

You are ruined.
>>> What will your life be?
>>>>>> Who will 'visit' your room?
Who uncover that beauty?
>>> Whom will you love?
>>>>>> Whose girl will you be?
Whom kiss?
>>> Whose lips bite?
>>>>>> Enough. Break.
Catullus.
>>> Against the past.

9

Veraniolus,
first of friends,
have you returned
to your own roof
your close brothers
& your mother
still alive? In-
deed it's true you're
back again &
safe & sound
among us all.
So now I'll watch
& listen to your
anecdotes of
Spanish men &
Spanish places
told as only
you can tell them.
I shall embrace
your neck & kiss
you on the mouth
& on the eyes,
Veraniolus. . . .

Of all light-hearted
men & women
none is lighter-
hearted than Cat-
ullus is to-day.

10

Alfenus Varus
buttonholes me
in the Forum
where I'm lounging,
drags me off to
view a girl who
seems at first a
not unlady-
like young lady,
of obvious 'charms'.
The small talk turns
on how Bithynia
stands – my luck there.
I answer (which is
true) that neither
locals, praetors,
nor their aides
make money, that
palm-greasing's out,
that Memmius,
our praetor, greased
his aides elsewhere.
"But you," they said
"were not so poor
"you couldn't run
"to litter slaves –
"they come from there."
And I, because
of her, said lightly:
"Things were bad, but

"not as bad as
"that – I'd eight stout
"porters." (I, who've
no one, here or
there, even to
lift the foot of
my split pallet.)
And the girl, in
character, at
once cooed: "Lend me
"your porters for
"an hour or two
"this afternoon –
"I feel like doing
"what girls do,
"at Serap's shrine."
"My dear," I said,
"of course, but act-
"ually they're Gaius
"Cinna's – not my own
"– he lets me use
"them when I want.
"It's all the same. . . .
"You really mustn't
"take your friend's friends
"at their word,
                          young lady,
"it's common as
"well as comic."

II

Furius, Aurelius, friends of my youth,
whether I land up in the Far East,
where the long-drawn roll of the Indian Ocean
      thumps on the beach,
or whether I find myself surrounded by Hyrcanians,
the supple Arabs, Sacians, Parthian bowmen,
or in the land where the seven-tongued Nile
      colours the Middle Sea,
whether I scale the pinnacles of the Alps
viewing the monuments of Caesar triumphant,
the Rhine, the outlandish seas of
      the ultimate Britons,
whatever Fate has in store for me,
equally ready for anything,
I send Lesbia this valediction,
      succinctly discourteous:
live with your three hundred lovers,
open your legs to them all (simultaneously)
lovelessly dragging the guts out of each of them
      each time you do it,
blind to the love that I had for you
once, and that you, tart, wantonly crushed
as the passing plough-blade slashes the flower
      at the field's edge.

12

While everyone else is laughing & drinking
you extend
      a surreptitious claw,
Asinius,
      towards the table napkins
of the negligent . . .
      an unattractive habit
you misguidedly think funny.
You demur?
      I assure you
it is at once squalid & unattractive.
Ask Pollionus, your brother
a boy crackling with wit
who would give a substantial sum
to disembarrass himself of your talents.
Expect, Asinius, a bombardo
of 300 hendecasyllables, or
return my napkin –
      of small value itself,
but a memory of friends,
      Veranius & Fabullus,
who sent this set of fine table linen
from Spain,
      a present cherished by Catullus
as his own Veraniolus –
as Fabullus mine – must always be.

13

I shall expect
you in to dine
a few days hence
Fabullus mine,
and we'll eat well
enough, my friend,
if you provide
the food & wine
& the girl, too,
pretty & willing.
I, Catullus,
promise you
wine & wit &
all the laughter
of the table
should you provide
whatever food
or wine you're able.
For, charmed Fabullus,
your old friend's purse
is empty now
of all but cobwebs!

In return, the
distillation
of Love's essence
take from me, or
whatever's more
attractive or
seductive than

Love's essence. For
Venus & her
Cupids gave my
girl an unguent,
this I'll give to
you, Fabullus, and
when you've smelt it
all you'll want the
gods to do is
make you one
gigantic nose
to smell it, always, with.

14

If, my irrepressible Calvus, I didn't
happen to love you more than my eyes
this hoax gift of yours would have made me
as cross as Vatinius. . . .
            What have I done to deserve
such (& so many) poets?
            I am utterly demoralised.
May the gods scowl on whoever
sent you this clutch of offenders
in the first place.
            – A grateful client?
I smell Sulla, the pedagogue.
A *recherché* & freshly culled volume,
such as this, could well come from his hands.
And that's as it should be – a meet &
acceptable sign that your efforts
(on his behalf) are not wasted.
But the collection itself is implacably bad.
And you, naturally, sent it along to Catullus
– your Saturnalian *bonne-bouche* –
so that Gaius, on this of all days,
might suffer the refinements of tedium.
No. Little Calvus. You won't run away
with this – for tomorrow, when the shops open,
I shall comb the bookstalls for Caesius, Aquinus,
Suffenus – all who excel in unpleasantness –
and compound your present with interest.
Until then, hence from my home, hence
by the ill-footed porter who brought you.
Parasites of our generation. Poets I blush for.

My love & I are yours to command
Aurelius –
            with the following 'modest' reservation:
if ever at any time you've held
a chaste good in your mind,
            unmarred by whatever desires,
modestly keep this boy of mine in like state.
I do not refer
            to the menace of common contacts,
to those set on their business
coming & going in the streets,
it is you
            & your punitive penis
I fear –
            a threat to all sorts & conditions of youth.
Wag this maleficent instrument
where, when & as much as you may
on whatever occasions occur
outside your domestic circle,
only withhold one item from its attentions. . . .
I present this modest request. But should
a congenital turpitude
            take you & prick you into
besetting Catullus's love with pitfalls of seduction
look for the luckless fate of the common adulterer:
he who
            with ankles clamped
and door open
            feels the horse-radish
(suitably cut for withdrawal)
            splitting him,
or the mullet's fins.

16

Pedicabo et irrumabo
Furius & Aurelius
       twin sodomites,
you have dared deduce *me* from my poems
which are lascivious
       which lack pudicity....
The devoted poet remains in his own fashion chaste
his poems not necessarily so:
       they may well be
lascivious
       lacking in pudicity
stimulants (indeed) to prurience
       and not solely in boys
but those whose hirsute genitalia are not easily moved.

You read of those thousand kisses.
You deduced an effeminacy there.
You were wrong. Sodomites. Furius & Aurelius.
Pedicabo et irrumabo vos.

Cologna Veneta –
    where the good folk
dancing & holding their games
    at *festa* time
on the rickety bridge over the Gua
have fears of the crazy bridge-props
(cast-outs from the lumber yard)
slithering one day
    (plop) in the river-mud
– a bargain!
    A risible ruse on my behalf,
and a new little bridge
    your own *ponte di Catullo*
where even the cavorting priests of Mars
can play leap-frog in safety. . . .
    Pray, pitch
headlong from your precarious perch
where the marish mud waits deepest
    & blackest
& infinitely offensive
    a Veronese acquaintance of mine.
The man is a boor. His reflexes less
than those of a snoozing baby
rocked in the crook of its daddy's arms.
His bride's in her first flowering . . .
    a girl as capricious
as a pampered yearling,
    one to be watched
as closely as the tenderest grape-cluster . . .
while he,

for less than a fig,
yields her her maidenhead games
            wherever she wants them.
Nor has he 'risen to the occasion'.
            Hamstrung
like a Ligurian alder
            – the chopper's child –
in a ditch by the roadside,
            he responds precisely as though
no woman were anywhere near him.
The fool
            hears nothing
sees nothing
            apparently knows nothing
(of himself included).
            Head over heels
from your little bridge
            despatch him
unawares –
            his dolt-like lethargy
traumatically stirred,
            who knows?
the husband may slough
            his horrid stupor
as the pack-mule casts
            its iron-soled slipper
in the obstinate mud.

18

I dedicate, I consecrate this grove to thee,
Priapus, whose home & woodlands are at Lampsacus;
there, among the coastal cities of the Hellespont,
they chiefly worship thee:
                their shores are rich in oysters!

21

Impresario of neediness
            to-day, to-morrow & of yesterday
Aurelius would openly stuff whom I love,
always with him
           laughing with him
'attached' to his flanks,
putting various tricks there to the test
– but in vain:
           schooled in your methods
I shall break you open (Aurelius) first. . . .
As a concomitance to good-living
           I acquiesce in your acts,
but when whom I love as honey,
           tastes your hunger
your thirst –
           preserve yourself. Desist.
You will attain your objective only
at the cost of being buggered by Catullus.

22

I must, Varus, tell you:
        Suffenus, known to us both as
a man of elegance, wit
        & sophistication
is also a poet
        who turns out verse by the yard.
No palimpsest copies
        but new books with new ivories
inscribed on Augustan Royal,
        the lines lead-ruled,
red tabs & red wrappers,
        the ends shaved with pumice.
But unwind the scroll
        & Suffenus
the well-known diner-out
        disappears.
A goatherd
        a country bumpkin
looks at us –
        strangely transmogrified.
What should one think?
        The envy of wits
becomes
        at the touch of the Muses
a bundle of gaucheries. . . .
        and he likes nothing better
fancies himself
        in the role of a poet. . . .
Yet who,
        in his own way,

[75]

is not a Suffenus?
> Each has his blind spot.
The moat & the beam.
> As Aesop says,
the pack on our own back
> that we don't see.

23

Friend Furius,
          'who has no slaves & no money' . . .
no bluebottle in the larder
          no spider
no bright hearth-fire,
          but a parent
& stepmother
          whose strong teeth
make short work
          of whatever you give them:
old boots & nails.
          Count yourself lucky –
your father, his lean spouse, yourself,
          in excellent health.
No indigestion.
          No fears of fire, flood & theft,
the usual bogies
          of prosperous householders.
(Who *could* want to poison you?)
          Your three bodies
like polished bone
          wonderfully dehydrated
by cold, heat & hunger,
          what more could you want?
Sweat, phlegm, saliva
          all nasal discharge
is foreign to you.
          You're as clean as whistles.
Even your arses, dry
          as fine, operative salt-cellars –

working
　　　maybe ten times a year,
the product
　　　like pebbles
or dry broad-beans
　　　easily friable
between the fingers
　　　& leaving no shit-smutch.
These blessings are not
　　　to be sneezed at.
You should count yourself lucky.
　　　You should also forgo
your importunate pleas
　　　for a 'small loan':
you've more than enough as it is
　　　– if you knew it.

24

Best sprig of the clan
   Iuventius
to-day, to-morrow, & of yesterday
rather you had bestowed the fortune
of Midas than your affections
on that man (Furius)
   'who has no slaves & no money'.
"But he is *acceptable*, surely?" you query.
   – Indeed,
& this 'acceptable' man has no slaves, no money.
Dispute or disparage the point as you will . . .

  (the man still has no slaves,
  he still has no money).

25

From Thallus the pederast
        of flesh flabbier
than rabbit fur
        gooseskin
                earlap
or the cobwebby penis of an elderly gentleman,
from Thallus the pederast
        as rapacious as
a typhoon in winter –
        its crop of gaping sailors,
I demand
        my Spanish scarves
                my scrolls from Bithynia
which you have abstracted
        and of which you are making
ridiculous display
        as of family heirlooms.
Release my belongings from your glutinous clutches
or those fleshy thighs
        those slug fingers
may carry the acute inscriptions of the 'cat',
and you, afflicted by unwonted sensations,
find yourself tossed hideously about
        – a cockle shell on winter sea.

꠸26

Your cottage, Furius, sheltered
from the dry Scirocco,
from Zephyrus,
                    from Apeliota,
from the bitter North-East draughts
is exposed to an *over*draft of a different sort –
£1,250:
        ghastly . . . ruinous.

27

Falernian,
        old Falernian!
cup-boy drown the cups
as custom of Postumia
tighter than the bursting grape
ordains
        but keep the water-jug
boon of the straight-faced
                        far hence
no friend to wine –
the Bacchus here is neat.

28

In Piso's suite
are empty pockets
empty trunks &
light equipage,
is that not so
Fabullus mine,
Veraniolus
best of friends?
Can you fill up
on his small beer?
can cash-books show
more gain than loss?
Or are you as
Catullus when,
a praetor's aide,
his cash-books showed
successive loss-
es, never gain?
Yes, Memmius, once
you filled me truly
slowly – daily –
with the length
of your great beam
and supine I
received it duly.
From what I see
your case is now
as mine was then:
you're stuffed with no
less large a crumb

of patronage. . . .
So, Veraniolus
& Fabullus
maledictions
on you both from
every Roman
god & goddess
for discredit
brought by you
upon the wolf-cubs
& their brood.

29

What man could stomach the sight
      that was not enthralled
by loot, lechery & the political game?
      Intolerable Mamurra
squanders
      what shaggy Gauls
what ultimate Britons
      once possessed.
Noblest Pederast!
      Your stomach remains unturned? . . .
You are enthralled by loot, lechery & the political game.
Overindulged & overweening
      the man stalks from bed to bed
like a white Venus–dove
      or a parody of Adonis.
Noblest Pederast!
      Does your stomach remain unturned? . . .
You are enthralled
      by loot, lechery & the political game.
Was this the reason for the British venture?
      That a debauched instrument
(yours & your son–in–law's)
      should gobble up all this money?
An unusual campaign . . .
      an unusual general!
Your celebrated munificence
      would appear to have been
'misplaced'. Has not enough coinage
      dribbled through this man's fist?
First his inheritance,

second the Pontic loot,
third, your own war in Spain,
         (the Tagus
where you washed for gold
         has a story of that),
& now Gaul,
         & now Britain,
shake in their shoes.
         Why keep him?
What is he good for –
         beyond treating the fattest endowment
as a comestible?
         Is this the reason
Rome's topmost tycoons,
         father-&-son-in-law,
have been playing billiards
         with our world?

30

Alfenus from Cremona
       forsakes the friendship of friends
friendless now
       quick to forget
              constant only in duplicity.
Gods of the Hill-Heavens do not smile on such acts,
a fact you ignore
       abandoning Catullus
fallen in sadness
       and ill.
              What can men do?
Where can a man hold fast?
       You commanded love
traduced my affections
       yielding no love-requital.
Now all is retracted,
       words, deeds,
dissolved under the clouds.
       You choose an eraser
but the gods will remember
       and Constancy also,
one day bringing the bitter herb to your mind.

31

Apple of islands, Sirmio, & bright peninsulas, set
in our soft-flowing lakes or in the folds of ocean,
with what delight delivered, safe & sound,
                                    from Thynia
from Bithynia
          you flash incredibly upon the darling eye.
What happier thought
         than to dissolve
the mind of cares
         the limbs from sojourning,
and to accept the down of one's own bed
under one's own roof
        – held so long at heart . . .

and that one moment paying for all the rest.

So, Sirmio, with a woman's loveliness, gladly
echoing Garda's rippling lake-laughter,
and, laughing there, Catullus' house
                    catching the brilliant echoes!

32

Call me to you
at siesta
we'll make love
my gold & jewels
my treasure trove
my sweet Ipsíthilla,
when you invite
me lock no doors
nor change your mind
& step outside
but stay at home
& in your room
prepare yourself
to come nine times
straight off together,
in fact if you
should want it now
I'll come at once
for lolling on
the sofa here
with jutting cock
and stuffed with food
I'm ripe for stuffing
                you,
my sweet Ipsíthilla.

33

Vibennius & son, renowned
among bath-hut pilferers

      père

an adept at 'massage'

       fils

of voracious if of hirsute buttocks
why not remove yourselves?
Those manual depredations
  are common knowledge,
the allurements of those bum-cheeks
  a drug on the market:
why not remove yourselves?

34

Moving in her radiant care
chaste men and girls moving
wholly in Diana's care
       hymn her in this.

Latona's daughter, greatest
of the Olympian race, dropped
at birth beneath the olive trees
       on Delian hills,

alive over mountain passes,
over green glades and
sequestered glens,
       – in the talkative burn,

Juno Lucina in the groans
of parturition, Hecat, fearful at crossed ways, the nymph
       of false moonlight.

You whose menstrual course
divides our year, stuff
the farmer's harvest barn
       with harvesting.

Sacred, by whatever name invoked
in whatever phase you wear, turn
upon our Roman brood, of old
       your shielding look.

35

Fetch, papyrus,
            our soft-measured poet
our *confrère* Caecilius
                down to Verona
fetch him down from the shores of Lake Como.
There are matters of moment a
mutual friend has to impart.
If you're wise you will swallow the miles
though a girl there calls back to you,
her blonde arms thrown round your neck
holding separation away . . .
who has been locked in desire
licked with the familiar flame
from the moment she first looked
at your new work – incomplete –
of the Great Mother
                the destructive Queen.

You, madam,
            — a Sappho *de nos jours*
have Catullus's sympathy,
Caecilius has indeed sung his incomplete song
of Cybele
            of her strong power over us all
with seduction.

36

Volusian sheets
shit-shotten Annals
discharge the pledge
that Lesbia makes
to Holy Venus
Holier Cupid:
– if I give
myself to her
alone, again,
discontinue
launching these
trucacious squibs,
on a pyre of
coffin chips she'll
burn the verses
of the meanest
Latin poet
read in Rome, a
votive blaze to
limping cuckolds. . . .
Thus with her
cerulean smile
has Lesbia pledged
a heavenly troth
in *trivia*. Hear,
Maid of sea-foam
Queen of Ancon
leafed Idalia
Cyprian Golgos
Amathusia

reed-bound Cnidos
Epidamnus
cross-roads of the
Adriatic,
take that vow as
here fulfilled and
neither lacking
wit nor point
in the performance:
burn script, blaze paper
into the fire you
rigmarole verse,
uncouth, banal
Volusian sheets,
shit-shotten Chronicle.

37

Nine posts, five doors, up the Clivus
              Victoriae, stands an
unsavoury resort . . . unsavoury
              habitués inside,
who think that only they have cocks,
              that only they can ruffle
a pudendum, the rest of us
              as apt as goats. I could
cheerfully bugger you all while
              you wait, kicking your heels.
Your numbers, a hundred or so,
              leave me undaunted. Think
of the man-power involved! And
              think of me now, scribbling
each of your names in black letters
              on the house-front. For she
whom once I loved as no other
              girl has been loved lives here.
Who has fled from my touch & sight.
              Whom I fought for & could
not keep. . . . A mixed bunch – successful,
              respectable men swap
places with dregs from the back-streets.
              She is open to all.
And one, who outdoes his home-grown
              rabbits – Egnatius,
the Spaniard with the beard, known for
              his wild dundrearies &
glistening teeth, assiduously
              (with native urine) scrubbed.

38

Angst,
       ennui & angst
consume my days & weeks,
and you have not written
or done anything to soothe my illness.
I am piqued.
       So much for our friendship.
Ah! Cornificius,
       a word from you would cure everything,
though more full of tears
       than a line from Simonides.

39

Because he has bright white teeth, Eg-
      natius whips out a
tooth-flash on all possible
      (& impossible) occasions.
You're in court. Counsel for defence
      concludes a moving per-
oration. (Grin.) At a funeral,
      on all sides heart-broken
mothers weep for only sons. (Grin.)
      Where, when, whatever the
place or time – grin. It could be a
      sort of 'tic'. If so, it's
a very *vulgar* tic, Egnatius,
      & one to be rid of.
A Roman, a Tiburtine or
      Sabine, washes his teeth.
Well-fed Umbrians & over-
      fed Etruscans wash theirs
daily. The dark Lanuvians
      (who don't need to), & we
Veronese, all wash our teeth. . . .
      But we keep them tucked in.
We spare ourselves the nadir of
      inanity – inane
laughter. You come from Spain. Spaniards
      use their morning urine
for tooth-wash. To us that blinding
      mouthful means one thing &
one only – the quantity of
      urine you have swallowed.

40

Whatever could have possessed you
to impale yourself on my iambics?
What ill-disposed deity inveigled you
Ravidus, into this one-sided contest?
Was it a letch for celebrity,
at no matter what cost?
                              – then you shall have it:
"Ravidus, loving in the place Catullus loves,
is lastingly nailed in this lampoon."

41

Formianus's whore,
                    long-nosed
well-stuffed Ameana,
claims that I owe her
'a cool thousand' – for *services*!

Gather round, friends & relations
call in the medical practitioners
assemble your kinsfolk
and place the girl under analysis.
Why?
        She is clearly the victim of hallucinations
        (an advanced case of psychosis).

42

From the quarters of the compass
       gather round Catullus
indelicate syllables
       as many as you are,
a slippery whore has caught
       Catullus by the hairs.
She won't give me my pocket book back.
Come with Catullus
       follow her along the sidewalk
accost her on her beat
       insist she gives it back.
You ask, "Which one is yours?"
       The one parading in front
like a stage tart
       grinning like a French poodle.
Surround the little bitch
       insist she gives it back:
  "My pocket book unwholesome whore
  unwholesome whore my pocket book."
She looks the other way.
       "O tart of turpitude! O brothel lees!"
The brazen-faced bitch does not blush.
Approach again
       repeat in even louder tones:
  "My pocket book unwholesome whore
  unwholesome whore my pocket book."
We make no visible impression.
       The girl is totally unmoved.
Indelicate syllables
       to get our pocket book

we must adopt a change of front
      we must adopt new tactics
thus:
    "Intact young lady and of nubile rectitude
    would you be so kind as
    to give me back my pocket book?"

43

O elegant whore!
      with the remarkably long nose
unshapely feet
      lack lustre eyes
fat fingers
      wet mouth
and language not of the choicest,
you are I believe the mistress
of the hell-rake Formianus.

And the Province calls you beautiful;
they set you up beside my Lesbia.
O generation witless and uncouth!

44

It depends who's talking if you're a 'Sabine'
        or 'Tiburtine' grange: hurtful people lay odds
you're 'Sabine', to friends 'Tiburtine' – but one or
        t'other, Catullus scuttles happily
to shake off a bronchial chill in your sub-
        urban grove, stomach-earned from lunging after
grandiose food-dishes. Dinner with Sestius
        has meant reading his appalling speeches (the
Antian case): cold, vapid, unpleasant – I
        was at once affected, displayed signs of chill,
developed a phlegmatic wheeze and fled
        to your safety, where with rest & nettle broth
a cure has been effected. Refreshed, my thanks
        to you my grange, not rubbing in this *bêtise*.
Next time I finger that maleficent script
        let Sestius himself be seized with 'flu & phlegm,
who invites Catullus solely to make him read
        speeches so bad no one else will touch them.

45

Phyllis Corydon clutched to him
her head at rest beneath his chin.
He said, "If I don't love you more
than ever maid was loved before
I shall (if this the years not prove)
in Afric or the Indian grove
some green-eyed lion serve for food."
      Amor, to show that he was pleased,
      approvingly (in silence) sneezed.
Then Phyllis slightly raised her head
(her lips were full & wet & red)
to kiss the sweet eyes full of her:
"Corydon mine, with me prefer
always to serve unique Amor:
my softer flesh the fire licks
more greedily and deeper sticks."
      Amor, to show that he was pleased,
      approvingly (in silence) sneezed.
So loving & loved so, they rove
between twin auspices of Love.
Corydon sets in his eye-lust
Phyllis before all other dust;
Phyllis on Corydon expends
her nubile toys, Love's dividends.
Could Venus yield more love-delight
than here she grants in Love's requite?

46

Now spring bursts
     with warm airs
now the *furor* of March skies
     retreats under Zephyrus . . .
and Catullus will forsake
     these Phrygian fields
the sun-drenched farm-lands of Nicaea
& make for the resorts of Asia Minor,
     the famous cities.
Now, the trepidation of departure
     now lust of travel,
feet impatiently urging him to be gone.
Good friends, good-bye,
     we, met in this distant place,
far from our Italy
     who by divergent paths
must find our separate ways home.

47

Lucius Calpurnius Piso Caesoninus
one circumcised Priapus of a proconsul
apparently prefers the company
       of a couple of society-mongers
Porcius & Socration
       his own mangy hirelings
to that of my dearest Veraniolus
my own dear Fabullus,
they dining well at the best places
you forced to hang about the street-corners
       angling for invitations.

48

Iuventius,
were I allowed
to kiss your eyes
as sweet as honey
on & on, three
thousand kisses
would not seem
too much for me,
as many as
ripe harvest ears
of sheaves of corn
would still not be
too much of kiss-
ing you, for me.

49

Silver-tongued among the sons of Rome
the dead, the living & the yet unborn,
Catullus, least of poets, sends
Marcus Tullius his warmest thanks:

- as much the least of poets
as he a prince of lawyers.

50

The other day we spent,
Calvus, at a loose end
flexing our poetics.
Delectable twin poets,
swapping verses, testing
form & cadence, fishing
for images in wine
& wit. I left you late,
came home still burning with
your brilliance, your invention.
Restless, I could not eat,
nor think of sleep. Under
my eyelids you appeared
& talked. I twitched, feverishly,
looked for morning . . . at last,
debilitated, limbs
awry across the bed
I made this poem of
my ardour & for our
gaiety, Calvus. . . . Don't
look peremptory, or
contemn my apple. Think.
The Goddess is ill-bred
exacts her hubris-meed:
lure not her venom.

51

Godlike the man who
sits at her side, who
watches and catches
    that laughter
which (softly) tears me
to tatters: nothing is
left of me, each time
    I see her,
. . . tongue numbed; arms, legs
melting, on fire; drum
drumming in ears; head–
    lights gone black.

Coda

Her ease is your sloth, Catullus
you itch & roll in her ease:

former kings and cities
lost in the valley of her arm.

Drop dead, Catullus, lie right down where you are & die.
That blister Nonnius occupies a magistrate's chair;
Vatinius commits perjury – & collects a consulate.
Drop dead, Catullus, just drop right down (& die).

53

I laughed. Calvus. I laughed today
when someone in the courtroom crowd, hearing
your quite brilliant *exposé* of
the Vatinian affair, lifted his hands up
in proper amazement, and cried suddenly:
"A cock that size . . . *and it spouts!*"
I laughed. Calvus. I laughed.

54

If not by all that his friends boast,
at least by pin-headed Otto's unattractive pate
by loutish Erius's half-washed legs
by Libo's smooth & judicious farts
by Sufficio's old man's lust turned green
may great Caesar be duly revolted. Once more
my naïve iambics strike home . . .

unique general!

55

Where
           if it's not too much to ask
are you hiding,
           Camerius?
I've searched for you in the circus
in the parks
           among the bookstalls
even in Church (!)
           I have accosted
on Pompey's Broadway
           tart after tart,
meeting
           as you would expect
with a succession of blank looks.
"Where's Camerius, you low-down whores?"
One opens her bodice,
"You could find him between these pink tits
if you looked."
           A job,
I reflected, for Hercules.

           Why, Camerius
why arrogate to yourself this scarcity value? . . .

If I were Europa's bronze jailer
doing my rounds in Crete,
if I were fleet Ladas
           or feather-footed Perseus,
if I rode the sky like Pegasus
or with the dazzling swiftness of Rhesus' team,

– supposing I had the sandals of all the winds
I should still find myself sapped dry
eaten with fatigue
        looking for you,
'friend'.
        Come, Camerius, out with it
bare your precious secret to the day –
where are we likely to find you?
who are these girls
        pliant as cream
who detain you?
        Remember,
to keep the tongue locked in the mouth
is to reject love's seasoning:
love-talk enhances love-acts.
Alternatively,
        if you want to,
bolt up your mouth . . .
        only
divulge to Catullus the whereabouts of this *amour*,
        so we may share her.

56

A matter for mirth, Cato, & a smile
worth your attention, you'll laugh
you'll laugh as you love your Catullus, Cato
listen – a matter for more than a smile!
Just now I found a young boy
       stuffing his girl,
I rose, naturally, and
         (with a nod to Venus)
fell and transfixed him there
with a good stiff prick,
           like his own.

57

Caesar Mamurraque!
A peerless pair of brazen buggers,
both tarred with the same brush
this, from the city
            that, from south Latium,
the stain ingrained no purgative can flush . . .
double dyed,
            the 'heavenly twins',
erudite in the skills of the one divan, each
as voraciously adulterous as the other –
joint competitors in the woman's market.
A peerless pair of brazen buggers!

58

Lesbia, our Lesbia, the same old Lesbia,
Caelius, she whom Catullus loved once
more than himself and more than all his own,
loiters at the cross-roads
                       and in the backstreets
ready to toss-off the 'magnanimous' sons of Rome.

59

Menenius' wife,
   a red-headed cat from Bologna,
cat-like licks-off Rufulus. . . .
You've seen her often
   in the public cemeteries,
scrounging for the food-offerings
   placed by the half-burnt bodies,
chasing the small loaves
   as they roll out of the fire,
and ducking a cuff
   from the unshaved corpse-heaver.

60

Hard. Hard. As she-cat whelped in desert mountains.
As Scylla's spawn spewed from the screaming vulvula.
As inhuman, precisely, as inflexible.

                                  So, the supplication that
rises to you fresh as the new chance
– is scorned. Hard. Hard.

61

Hill (breeder) of Helicon,
        sun's seed of Urania,
        magnet a man is
for a maiden,
            Hymenaeus Hymen Io!
        Io! Hymen Hymenaeus.

Soft smell of marjoram
        melt on your forehead,
        cast the flame veil
come, joyfully:
        upon a white foot
                the saffron shoe.

Gaiety of daybreak!
            ringing voices
        shake out the bride-song!
        dance-throb in the fields,
tossing the pine torch,
        arms, waving.

Vinia comes to her altar,
        stands to her Manlius,
        shining as Venus to Paris,
rare fortune is born
        of a rare girl,

fair as the flowering Hamadryads
        or the myrtle they tend
        as their toy,

the shaft
shining,
wet with their dew.

Come, Hymen! come from your hill slopes
come from Aonian cave
from the Thespian rock
leave your cold nymph,
Aganippe,
– leave her her waters,

come! bring the bride home
set her, passionate,
beneath her new yoke
lock her up in her love
as the tree
fast in its ivy.

And you, girls innocent
of men,
whose own bride-day comes
come! shake out the bride-song:
'Hymenaeus Hymen Io!
Io! Hymen Hymenaeus.'

Happily cleaving the aether
the god's presence
descending
Hymen will answer your calls:
leading in Venus,
her bounties,
he couples true lovers.

Where else can the lover,
   tortured, turn?
   what greater god among men?
Hymenaeus Hymen Io!
   Io! Hymen Hymenaeus.

Trembling, the father
     hands you his daughter,
   for you, she'll unfasten
   her girl's girdle,
for your step, the bridegroom
   swollen with love, waits.

You pluck the flower
   from the mother's lap,
   in the novice's hand
the spray blossoms,
     Hymenaeus Hymen Io!
   Io! Hymen Hymenaeus.

There are no love-games,
   fairly played,
     without you,
   but with you
Venus luxuriates,
   where is your match among gods?

Absent, our homes
   are empty of children,
   parents barren of offspring,
with you –
   they proliferate!
   what greater god among gods?

[123]

Destitute of your sanctities
            the land is defenceless
            with you
she is inviolate,
            where is your match among gods?

Fling the doors wide
            she has come!
            See
                a shower
of torch flakes. . . .

    .   .   .   .

    .   .   .   .

            bashfully holds back,
            and steps
                hesitant
towards the threshold
            in tears –

no tears! Aurunculeia,
            the bright day will not see
            a more beautiful woman
than you
            spring from the sea:

a hyacinth of flowers,
            apart in a great garden,
            'a rich man's flower':
you linger: the day fades,
            shed your concealment!

[124]

Shed your concealment!
   a new bride
   hear our bride-speech,
see, the shower of torch flakes!
   shed your concealment!

No fickle lusts,
   no rooting between
   other sheets –
your husband will lie
   only in the valley of your breasts,

a 'hero' caught in your arms
   as the grape pole
   caught in the twisting vine.
See! the day fades:
   shed your concealment!

O bed in which all. . . .
  . . . .
  . . . .
  . . . .

   and at the white foot of the bed.

Venus will shine for him
   in the vague night,
   blaze
    at mid-day.
The day fades:
   new bride, shed your concealment!

Toss the pine torches!
   see, the flame

veil approaching,
shake out the bride-song!
Hymenaeus Hymen Io!
Io! Hymen Hymenaeus.

Ribaldry of marriage
and nuts
nuts
for the scrambling boys,
friend!
that sort of love is finished,

a cascade of nuts!
listless you may be:
you've played with nuts
in your time
now Talasius waits on your service,
a cascade of nuts!

No servant girl to his taste
or to yours
until now
(and the barber scrapes your first hairs)
come,
a cascade of nuts!

Does the 'well dressed groom'
letch
after former smooth cheeks?
– *that* sort of love is over,
Hymenaeus Hymen Io!
Io! Hymen Hymenaeus.

[126]

Yours were the licensed joys,
        but the licence
                expires
with your marriage,
Hymenaeus Hymen Io!
        Io! Hymen Hymenaeus.

And Lavinia, let your man ride
        how he will – where he will,
        or you'll find him riding elsewhere,
Hymenaeus Hymen Io!
        Io! Hymen Hymenaeus.

The *châtelaine*
        of a fine house,
        dispenser of influence,
Hymenaeus Hymen Io!
        Io! Hymen Hymenaeus,

until, white with woman's age
        the old head
        quivers all day
in endless assent,
            Hymenaeus Hymen Io!
        Io! Hymen Hymenaeus.

Now, in the saffron shoe,
                with fair omens,
        step over the threshold
        approach the porch doors,
Hymenaeus Hymen Io!
        Io! Hymen Hymenaeus.

Within, stretched on the Tyrian couch
        your one man
        swelling with love
waits for you only,
            Hymenaeus Hymen Io!
      Io! Hymen Hymenaeus.

A withering flame
        stirs in him
           as in you,
      but his the deeper,
less radiant, heat,
            Hymenaeus Hymen Io!
      Io! Hymen Hymenaeus.

Page, let go
        the bride's arm
        let her come
to her bride-bed,
            Hymenaeus Hymen Io!
      Io! Hymen Hymenaeus,

and you women,
        practised in bride-bed
        and birth-bed
           disarray her
bring her to Hymen,
            Hymenaeus Hymen Io!
      Io! Hymen Hymenaeus.

Now Manlius stands at the bed
        where she waits

        shining
      a lily among yellow field-flowers:
she lies,
        white on the saffron sheets.

But Manlius has
        his own love-gifts
        Venus has blessed him:
come, do not linger –
        the day fades,

and he comes, straight to the bedhead,
        with Venus inside him
        he takes his desire
in full view:
        love knows no concealments.

Assessing their love is like counting
        the stars in the sky
        or the sands
in the African desert:
        theirs are a hundred love games.

Play out your love games
        freely and swiftly
        plant the new shoot
an old name cannot lapse
        you must make, in the one place,
                      constant renewal.

May a diminutive Torquatus
        drop from Lavinia's womb

waving pink arms
with a smile (first)
         for his father,

whose stamp he must carry
         plain to the world,
         the bond
of his mother's
         fidelity,

and Lavinia will rank
         with Penelope,
         chaste in the birth
of Telemachus:
         archetype of wives.

Fold the doors softly,
         bridesmaids,
         feasting is over,
let them ply arms and legs
                  in their love-games,
         the constant renewal.

62

Young Men

Gather young men as the twilight gathers
       Vesper gleams faintly in heaven
it is time to bestir
       time to abandon the wedding tables
for the bride comes through the dusk
       it is time for the bride-hymn.
    Hymen Hymenaeus attend O Hymen!

Maidens

Watch where the young men gather by the porch-doors
face them while Vesper hangs fire over Thessaly
they are gathering quickly
       intent on their song
on contesting the bride-song with us
       response versus response.
    Hymen Hymenaeus attend O Hymen!

Young Men

Here is no palm for the asking
       observe these
young girls conferring together with girlish seriousness,
their care
       a sole-minded intensity
must
       produce the worth while,
while we
       distracted
deserve our defeat
       our minds on the one thing

[131]

with only an ear for the song:
        success waits on devotion.
Come! bend minds to the business
        girls flower in song
        man makes response.
    Hymen Hymenaeus attend O Hymen!

Maidens

What flame glows more pitilessly in heaven than yours
Vesper:
        under your gaze
the daughter wrenched from her mother's clasp,
        from the mother's clasp
twined there
        torn apart
her maidenhead placed under a young man's burning hand:
what jackbooting of lost cities
        pitiless as such an act?
    Hymen Hymenaeus attend O Hymen!

Young Men

What flame shines more resplendently in heaven than yours
Vesper:
        under your sign the marriage bond is sealed
the young man's troth
        the father's pledge
is effected
        in your ardour the consummation is joined:
what hour from the gods
        resplendent as such an hour?
    Hymen Hymenaeus attend O Hymen!

Maidens

Vesper has bereft us of one. . . .

.   .   .   .   .

Young Men

With your rising
       the night watchman guards against
furtive lovers on the prowl by night
       whom you as Lucifer
may disconcertingly discover
       still at their thefts
for maidens' acts belie their mock complaints,
affecting aversion
       for what they most desire.
     Hymen Hymenaeus attend O Hymen!

Maidens

When withdrawn in some walled garden
       a rose blooms
safe from the farm plough
       from farm beasts
strong under sun
       fresh in light free air
sprouting in rain showers
that rose is beauty's paragon for man or woman's pleasure,
but once the bud has blown
       – when the thin stalk is left
no paragon remains for man or woman's pleasure:
so, intact
       a girl stays treasured of her sex
but let her lose her maidenhead
       her close petals once polluted

[133]

she cannot give the same delight again to men
            no longer be the cynosure of virgins.
      Hymen Hymenaeus attend O Hymen!

Young Men

When in an open field
            unyoked a vine droops
no vine-limbs shake to the wind
            no ripe grape-clusters sprout
there the soft plant stoops under its own weight
           the vine-tips flop to their roots
that vine no hind nor husbandman will husband,
but yoke her to her elm-pole mate
and hinds & husbandmen in droves will husband her:
so, intact
           a girl grows withered in her sex
but yoke her to her mate in her ripe season
she will yield her parents ease
          she will yield delight to men.
      Hymen Hymenaeus attend O Hymen!

Young Men & Maidens

Resign as your father resigns you to this man
strength lies in surrender
          father & mother in concert
resign you,
          incline to their will
remember your
own maidenhead is not truly your own
          one part to your father
one to your mother
          only a third to yourself

incline then to their will & consign
>your share as they theirs
with the bride-gift,
>to this man
>in wedlock.
>>Hymen Hymenaeus attend O Hymen!

63

Plunging towards Phrygia over violent water
shot on the wood-slung Berecynthian coast
Attis with urgent feet treads the opaque ground
of the Goddess, his wits fuddled, stung with phrenetic
itch, slices his testicles off with a razor-
flint, sees the signs of new blood spotting
the earth, knows arms, legs, torse, sans
male members and
                    SHE
ecstatically snatches in delicate hands
the hand-drum of Cybebe, the hand-drum
of forest rites and Cybebe's torture
with nervous fingers taps the hollowed hide
shakes it and shaking summons the Mother's Brood:
"Ololugmos!
                To Cybebe's thickets!
                                You have found the strange coast.
Ololugmos!
                Stamp in my footprints!
                                You are tied to my tether.
Ololugmos!
                Capsized in my currents –
                                    unsexing yourselves
in my Love-hate.
                Ololugmos! Break the close thicket,
with rabid abandon brighten Dindymia's face
stamp on Cybebe's ground
                                stamp where the drum shudders
stamp where the cymbals clang
                                where the flute drones

where the Maenads convulsively toss their ivied heads
where the protracted scream signals the Maenad rite –
the carlines flit restlessly in the grove
– Come with your quick triple step,
                              Ololugmos!"
As Attis speaks
              the trembling tongues of her neophytes
rise with the drum beats,
                        the concave cymbals begin clanging.
They head for green Ida.
                    Attis is a frenzied steer.
She gasps
     goaded by yoke-hate
bursts through the holy grove,
                        the throbbing drums
the foot-mad Gallae, stream in her wake. . . .
And the touch of Cybebe's bower brings lassitude.
Fatigue lowers their lids. They are foodless.
Investing apathy unstrings the manic pitch.
They sleep.
        Then when the sun's manifold hooves splinter
darkness, and the eyes from the gold mask sweep sky &
   earth
& the wild sea, Sleep takes a nimble dive from waking Attis into the expectant arms of his paramour
                              – Pasithea.
At once, shedding the night's tranquillity, Attis
relives the pictures in her heart,
                        freed from the maelstrom,
unclouded, recognises the rootless place where she has
   come,
her thoughts turned inside out, goes headlong back

to the beach, where she cries to Attica she has lost
for ever . . . looks over the brutal water
that stares back at her through her tears:
"Attica mother & maker, I
like a grateless housecarl fleeing
his mesne, footloose among Ida's
snows among the wood & rock lairs
with the boar caves for an icy hearth,
have I stripped myself of my patrimony
friends, goods, kin?
                  Are these ungreek landscapes
my new life-home?
               Where is Attica?
Where can the pupil open with Attica?
The storm has lifted
             and there is no *piazza,*
where is the stadium? the wrestling ring? the gymnasium
– a fallen life left to tread sorrow.
What have I not known? What shape not been?
A synthetic woman:
                once man, once lad, once boy.
Once the flower of the athletes.
                Once the pride of the young wrestlers.
My doors & thresholds were warm with friends.
The house full of blossoms greeting
the morning separation from the lover's couch.
And now, I, but part 'I',
               a plucked torse
a Maenad
     familiar of the gods
              huscarl of Cybebe,
tethered under these obsessive peaks

rooting with the tree-stag & the boar
                                    in the snow woods,
the pain at Attis' heart outweighs the Attis rage."
As the words fly from the pink mouth
they lodge in Cybebe's ears
who stoops to the fear-of-flocks
unyokes the left-hand lion
and whispers:
            "Attis is truant. Hound Attis hither.
Infect her with fear & desire
for Cybebe's pale. Lash at yourself with
your tail-knot. Drown the whole mountain
with roaring. Let the red mane dreadfully
cloud the brute neck."
                    She looses the leash.
The beast self-scourges its flanks
bounds through the brushwood, bursts
on the white-lined sands, appearing
where delicate Attis still stands by the sea.
The demented creature flees to Cybebe's wold
her life-space doomed spent in Cybebe's thrall.

"Great Cybebe, Mother Goddess, Berecynthian Queen,
avert your fury from Catullus' house
goad others to your actions,
others trap in the snarl of frenzy."

64

In old days
                    driving through soft waters
to the River of Pheasants
                    to the end of the Euxine Lake
pines sprung from Pelion
                    carrying picked men
Argives each like a tree
                    hearts set on the Colchian pelt
of gold, daring to track
                    salt deserts in a fast ship
cutting blue waves with firwood blades
for whom the indweller of the arx
                    the queen of hill-castles
had made hull poop & sail
                    – volatile under light winds –
binding firmly the pine-plaits to the curved underprow
the first boat to experience innocent sea –
Amphitrite.
                    As the moving waves took the keel
the water, chopped with oars, grew white
and from the runnels of foam faces peered
of Nereids, wondering. Then
and not since
                    men with their own eyes
 saw the bare bodies of nymphs
                    in broad daylight
caught in the marbled runnels of foam
as far down as the nipples. . . .
So Peleus was stirred towards Thetis
so Thetis came to a woman's bridal

and Jove gave his blessing.
                              O heroes
brides nymphs oreads
                born in a golden time
before the tribe of gods had gone from earth
I call on you in my poem
                standing with Peleus
Pillar of Thessaly
                blest beyond most in their bride-torches
whom Jove himself
                author of gods and goddesses
has given one of his girls,
                and Thetis
prettiest of mermaids
                touched as her own,
whom Tethys & old Ocean
                girdling all that we stand on –
have yielded a granddaughter.
                On the day
the longed-for light leaps up
Thessaly gathers in concourse
                gift-bearing guests
a laughing crowd
                their hearts in their faces
converge on the Palace.
                Cieros is empty
Phthiotic Tempe deserted
                the houses in Crannon
Larissa's walls
                abandoned –
flocking into Pharsalia
                packed under Pharsalian roofs

the crowds gather.
>   No man tills the field
the bullock's neck grows soft.
>   Not for many days shall the pronged hoe
rake among the vine-roots,
>   or the pruning hook lessen
the olive tree's deep shade.
>   Oxen do not turn the lumps of loam,
>   red rust flakes the neglected plough.
But in the royal halls
>   wherever you look
as room unfolds into room
>   silver & gold gleam
an effulgence of ivory,
>   carved thrones,
glittering cups on the long tables
the whole building thrums with the splendour of royal
        goods,
and there, in the middle,
>   inlaid with Indian tooth
and quilted with arras,
>   the divan of the small goddess
>   the arras ochred with rock-lichen &
>   tinctured with stain of rose shell-fish.

This quilt is pricked
>   with figures of gods & men
sketches of antiquity in *petit point*!
Here are the never-silent sands of Naxos
here Theseus vanishes towards the north,

a woman watches from the empty beach
                    unflagging grief in her heart,
Ariadne doesn't yet believe, quite,
                    she is witnessing what her eyes see –
she's only just woken from a trap
(of sleep)
        found herself alone on the island.
And Theseus, heedless as storm & wind
                    carves up the waves as he goes
and throws their love-words overboard.
                    But the Minoan girl
with seaweed on her legs
                    goes on looking from the shallow water
with tragic eyes
                    she goes on looking from a long way
frozen in the statuary of grief,
                    like a Maenad,
until waves of her own shake her
                    her hair shakes loose of her yellow snood
her thin bodice flaps open at her breasts
her breasts, the colour of milk,
                    push through her torn brassière,
snood skirt bra
                    the shallows take her torn clothes
swirling the silk in eddies at her ankles
the clothes do not matter:
                    her body is lost in you
Theseus –
                    Ariadne!
Venus has kept for you her best thorn of love
love-fated girl
                    love-fated from the hour Theseus

[143]

steered from the curved breakwater of the Piraeus
set course for the iron city of the iron king
Minoan Knossos.

       A blight lay over the narrow streets of Athens. . . .
The story goes that to absolve herself
of the murder of the bull-king's son
                  Androgeos
at the games at the Panathenaea
       Athens yielded
yearly ten of her best men
yearly ten nubile girls (unmarried)
       food for the bull-king
until Prince Theseus one day
       proffered himself for his sweet city,
"The shipments of the dead not dead
from here to Crete shall stop".
He sailed in a good ship, before fine winds,
coming to the rock-hewn halls of Knossos.
From her window
       the royal girl looked down
with a girl's lust,
       whom the women's quarters enfolded
in her chaste bed
       as petals the scented stamen
who was like the myrtle buds on the banks of the Eurotas
or the coloured breath of springtime
not lifting her hot eyes
         till fire ran in her womb –
       the girl's body swathed in fire.
Remorseless Cupid

Holy Child
      – who stirs hate & love in one cup!
Venus of Eryx
      – a girl who will drown in your floods
      whispering at a blond stranger!
Venus of Golgos
      – and expectations breaking in the heart!
Venus of leafy Idalia
      – how often the girl's cheeks – sallow, like gold!
As Theseus walked out to meet the beast
poised between death and celebrity
Ariadne addressed herself to her prayers
           with firm lips
making her small offerings to the gods,
who acted.
      For as on the top of Mount Taurus
in Turkey
      where the great oaks shake out their boughs
and the pine trees drip resin
      a high wind contorting the trunk
can pluck out a tree by its roots
      so that the monster upended
comes down beamwise
      splintering what's in its path
so Theseus capsized the bull-monster
      and the quelled body lay in a heap
its fruitless horns sticking up.
      Then fingering the thread
he turned his feet back,
      along the delusive maze
of palace corridors,
      stepped out of the labyrinth

a hero, unharmed
            and made off with the girl
- prizing sweet love & Theseus
            before the lot of them
eluding her father's watch
forgoing her three sisters' embraces
                            her mother's,
tearful for a lost daughter
whom the wind blew to white-ringed Naxos
whom sleep took in the night
whom yesterday's bridegroom
                            forsworn
left, before morning.

            And now scared at her own grief
scattering her screams broadside
                she runs to the top of the cliffs
looks at the waves rolling northwards
then runs out into the sea
                holding her silk petticoat above her knees,
glass-cheeked,
        at the end of tears,
        and frozen with tears,
the words well from the pit of her bride's stomach:

"Why did you lift me from Cretan bower
"dumping me here on an empty beach,
"shrugging off Heaven, her plans for us,
"heedless of freighting home snapped pledges?
"Nowhere the means to flex steel

[146]

"no appeal that could touch you.
"You did not tell me to look for seduction
"but for bride-ale & wedding torches,
"for the increments of Hymen,
"– waste words shredded now on wind.
"Now no woman listen to man's love-words
"or look to find there his love-bond:
"as long as they itch for it
"they will say anything
                    do anything,
"but with lust slaked
         "the soft words are forgotten
         "the promises null.
"I caught you from the back coil of your fate
"happy to exchange a half-brother for love's need
"and you leave me – scavenge for island birds & beasts:
         "no tumulus for me dead
         "no death-dust as cover.
"You are flint
              where the bitch-cat whelps under desert rock,
"or spume
         when brine-water sickens with sea-spawn,
"you are the kindless issue of the twin gulfs
                              – storm-ridden Syrtes –
"of the octopus & the maelstrom,
                         epitomes of ruin.
"Is this your guerdon for a life saved?
"If you did not want to marry me
"because of your father (who is prejudiced)
"you could have taken me home with you
"and I should have tended you
"got your bath ready for you,

"washing your arms & feet with spring water,
"each day smoothing the coloured bedspread in your
    room.
"But why should I give my tears
"to this wind? In this state?
"Wind is deaf as well as dumb.
"And he's wind-driven in the middle distance.
"There's nothing here but rocks & seaweed.
"In the hubris of indifference Fate
"deprives me even of an ear to listen.
"If only the Athenian sloop
"had never entered the bay
"at Knossos, with its grim cargo
"for the bull, fixed hawsers to the quay,
"captained by an attractive sailor . . .
"with a soul like a trap-door
"whom we took in out of pity –

                            his name was Theseus.
"Where can I go?
                    What is left for me?
"Our Cretan hills?
                    There's bitter water between.
"A father?
                Whom I abandoned in blood guilt.
"Or the love-purpose of a husband?
"Who makes the rowlocks creak
"in his hurry to get away from me.
"And inland on Naxos?
                        Derelict
"no roof-tree
            no escape
"the surcingle of sea-water

"no hope
          no reason for refuge
"all is dumb
          all is alone
                    all is nothing
"but these lids won't grow grubby with death
"till from the gods I've wrung amercement –
"on Olympus someone tips back the scales.
"Listen:
          raveners of men's evil
                              Erinyes
"upon whose scalps
                    as images of hate
"snakes feed,
          Tisiphone!
                    Megaera!
"Alecto!
          these moans are forced
"from a feverish body,
"as blind as epilepsy,
"they are the truth of Ariadne's heart.
"Don't waste what galls,
"make Theseus deal
"as brutally as he dealt me
"himself & someone loved."

As the voice poured from the tragic mouth
crying for revenge on the ill dealt her
Jove's brow bent in assent
so that land and wild sea shook,
the gleaming stars shivered in the sky

and a mist fell on Theseus
who at once forgot the strict words,
till then locked in his heart,
that he signal careworn Aegeus
by hoisting the glad-omened sails
when the home port hove in sight.
For before Theseus slipped anchor
dropping beneath the city's ramparts
his father had kissed him
yielding his son to sea-winds
with the words:

"Restored at the tail-end of my life
"from Troezene, my only Theseus
"dearer than years to your father
"of whom Fate & your own zest
"would rob him a second time,
"even before his failing eyes
"had gotten used to your face,
"I despatch you without happiness
"banning bravado of flags & auguries.
"I make public grief
"with dust & ash on my grey hair
"and the dark canvas hung
"from your voyaging mast:
"Hibernian dyed purple
"signal of foreboding.
                            But should Athene
"shield of Athens & of Athenians
"stoop to sprinkle your right hand
"with the bull's blood, enact closely

[150]

"heart-kept, unflecked by time
"this mandate:
          On sight of Attic hills
"to strip ship of purple
"& hoist white sails from the plaited cords
"so Aegeus, at the first, may see
"with carefree heart his son safe,
"Theseus bent homeward in bright-omened hour."

But these words locked in intention
drifted from Theseus' head
as the wind imperceptibly lifts
the snow-mist from the hill-tops.
For Aegeus posted himself in the watch-tower,
his eyes tear-gutted,
he saw the dark shrouds
he read the false news of death
and the old king cast himself from the battlements,
while the boy, fresh from the bull-killing
'came home' – entered a stricken palace
victim of deceit as grim
as he off Naxos coast had sprung
bewildered Ariadne –

          . . . who still gazes where the hull has dwindled,
who revolves in her bride's heart a maze of sorrow.

                    And elsewhere on the quilt
flushed with desire for the Minoan bride

[151]

Bacchus his crew
of Satyrs & Silenes
descend about the glittering god,
from Ethiopia, from Ind, from Thrace
with tossing heads
with frenzied 'Evoes!'
they are shaking the thyrsus
shaking the vine leaves round it,
they catch the torn bits of bullock
the snake belt writhes at their hips
and the secret *cartouche*
hiding the sacred objects
objects no common sight profanes
passes to the hand-slap drum beat,
bagpipe, horn & cymbals
sprinkle the hillside with discordant music.

Such the stitches worked in the wedding quilt,
such the splendid figures embracing the divan.
The young guests from Thessaly
their eyes filled with the tapestry
gradually ebb
from courts & corridors,
the demi-gods are due:
it is a dawn figure,
Aurora climbs
to the threshold of the day-sojourning sun,
Zephyr
flicks the flat water into ridges
with a morning puff,
the sloped waves

loiter musically,
             later the wind rises
& they rise,
             they multiply,
they shed the sun's sea purple as they flee.
In this way
             the crowd scatters from the royal crannies,
the mortal guests disperse to their own homes.

And now, Chiron,
             first to arrive,
carrying from Mount Pelion
             green gifts
of Thessalian buds
             from fields & alps
from river banks
             where the light west wind
has unsealed them.
             It is the centaur's *potpourri*.
They luxuriate
             through the wedding rooms
with a confused fragrance.
             And behind Chiron,
Peneus
             bearded with rushes
from Tempe
             whose girdling woods
are a river roof.
             He brings
store of beech
             dripping roots,

& laurel
  like a girl's flanks,
he brings the plane tree
  that is restless,
the piercing cypress
  & the poplar
supple in the wind,
  its tears of amber
for flame-shrouded Phaeton.
  The river god
heaps the foliage
  outside & in
until the house
  is dressed
for a bride's bower-bed.
  Next, Prometheus
patron of crafts
  & seer
still showing
  the faint cicatrices
Jove's penance
  paid on the cliff-face
in Caucasus,
  rock-chained
arms & legs
  thirty years. . . .
And then follows Jove,
  Juno,
their issue –
  only Apollo
the archer
  & his twin sister, Artemis,

have spurned
            the bride-ale & wedding torches
and are left to haunt Heaven.

The gods have disposed
            their white forms
at the wedding tables.
            It is bride-hymn time.
The Parcae prepare
            to intone
the prophetic song.
            The white shift
wrapping their palsy
            is alive,
it is red-hemmed
            at the ankles,
and their white hair
            is bound
with a red cloth.
            Their deft fingers
manipulate
            the eternal thread,
one hand on the distaff
            the other carding
with upturned fingers
            the spindle wool,
drawing the thread
            downwards,
twirling the whorl
            as the thread lengthens,

[155]

and stooping
      with mauve lips
to bite the rough ends off
      so that the bits hang
from the withered skin.
      An osier basket bulges
with new-shorn fleece . . .
      the wool whirrs
and the clear voices ring
      in Epithalamion
for Thetis,
      her bride-doom
time-sealed.

"Emathian bulwark, son of Jove,
whose acts augment his born worth,
accept the sisters' wedding truth.

Inexorably, fate follows thread,
from spindle to the shuttle running.

Fair-fortuned star that draws the bride
to groom, that yields the longed-for wife
whose mastery of love will drown
his heart, who settling to the drawn-
out marriage sleep will make her arms
light cushions for his heavy neck.

Inexorably, fate follows thread,
from spindle to the shuttle running.

Not yet such love as Peleus
for Thetis holds (& she for him)
has been – or such a grove of love.

Inexorably, fate follows thread,
from spindle to the shuttle running.

A child, Achilles, void of fear:
foe known face-on not fleeing, first
in racing, in hunt fleeter than
the fleet-foot stag, whose hooves strike flame.

Inexorably, fate follows thread,
from spindle to the shuttle running.

No warrior dare confront Achilles
where the Trojan rivers stream with
Trojan blood, and the Greeks raze stone
from stone of Troy, ten years consumed.

Inexorably, fate follows thread,
from spindle to the shuttle running.

The women at the gravesides weep
his deeds, their hair is loose, coated
with ash-dust, their ageing bosoms
showing fist marks of their sorrow.

Inexorably, fate follows thread,
from spindle to the shuttle running.

As the farmer's scythe in close-packed
cornstalks, stripping the yellow field,
his fierce blade crops Troy's men-at-arms.

Inexorably, fate follows thread,
from spindle to the shuttle running.

Scamander by quick Hellespont
will watch his valour swell, its width
shrink with slaughter-stooks, while its deep
course warms with the issuing blood.

Inexorably, fate follows thread,
from spindle to the shuttle running.

And Polyxena, death-given,
too shall watch . . . and watch the earth-tomb
rise, where her maiden limbs will fall.

Inexorably, fate follows thread,
from spindle to the shuttle running.

Once Chance lets slip the Greeks inside
the sea-born belt of stone, the young
girl's blood will soak the barrow mound,
who crouches to the two-edged sword
& pitches, a headless trunk, forward.

Inexorably, fate follows thread,
from spindle to the shuttle running.

But now the joining of their loves,
as Peleus accepts his nymph, &
Thetis lightly yields to wedlock.

Inexorably, fate follows thread,
from spindle to the shuttle running.

And dawn light finds the nurse who tries
today's neck-fillet, her mother reads
the sign & smiles: the goddess was
not coy in love – young fruit will follow.

Inexorably, fate follows thread,
from spindle to the shuttle running."

This song
            of happy wedding-fates
the Parcae sang
            to Peleus
in old days.
            For once
when piety had place on earth
            the gods themselves
stood at our chaste doors
            or drank at the bride-ales
of mortal heroes.
            On Holy Feasts
Jove from his bright throne
saw the earth littered with a hundred bulls.
The wine-god on Parnassus
            goading his dishevelled troop

was hailed
      with altar smoke
from happy Delphos
      where the rasping Thyiades
had emptied street & square.
      Athene, Mars or Artemis
appeared
      in the death-tussle
and lit men's hearts.
      To-day ill wreaking rules.
Man's piety is fled.
   The loveless child neglects its parent's death
   a brother's blood trickles from brothers' hands
   the first son's girl attracts the father's lust
   who seeks a step-dame & a son's demise
   unwittingly the youngster mounts his mother
   her vicious incest spurning the house-kin
   spirits: laws bouleversé, and the welter
   such, those of Hill-Heaven have withdrawn their care.

No longer do they deign
to keep our bride-ales, or
reveal themselves to us
in the light of common day.

Although entangled in prolonged grief
severed from the company of the Muses
and far from Pieria
        my brain children still-born
myself among Stygian eddies
the eddies plucking at the pallid foot
of a brother
        who lies under Dardanian soil
stretched by the coastland
        whom none may now hear
none touch
        shuttered from sight
whom I treasured more than this life
and shall –
        in elegies of loss
plaintive as Procne crying under the shadow of the
  cypress
for lost Itylus,
        I send, Hortalus, mixed with misery
Berenice's Lock –
        clipped from Callimachus
for you might think my promise
had slipped like vague wind through my head
or was like the apple
        unavowed
the girl takes from her lover
        thrusts into her soft bodice
and forgets there . . .
        till her mother takes her off guard –
she is startled,

the love-fruit trundles ponderously across the
  floor
and the girl, blushing, stoops gingerly
                                    to pick it up.

66

Who scans the bright machinery of the skies
& plots the hours of star-set & star-rise,
this or that planet as it earthward dips,
the coursing brightness of the sun's eclipse,
who knows the dreams that fill Endymion's head
& draw sly Cynthia to his Latmian bed –
palace astronomer, whose gaze is set
more earnestly on Heaven than on *Debrett*,
by you this soft effulgence first was seen
who knew at once the ringlets of the Queen,
those ringlets Berenice with bridal care
pledged when the King left for the Syrian war
(the suppliant Queen with tender arms outspread
the King still swollen from the marriage bed),
who carries with him marks of sweeter strife,
the night's clear traces of a virgin wife!
      Are brides averse to Venus (as they show)
or are their tears transparencies of woe
brilliantly shed amidst the wedding scene
effective bar to *you know what I mean?*
Their tears are false. I saw a bride's tears shed
when wartime took her husband from her bed.
Still wedded to the Queen's resplendent hair
I witnessed Berenice's crude despair.
And does she wail a so-called 'brother' gone,
or that she lies in bed at night alone,
her body wasted with intensive fire,
her soul devoid of all save one desire?
The proof is here, for virgin she displayed
a spirit commoner in man than maid.

When her betrothed preferred her mother's charms
she saw him slain, couched in Apáme's arms,
procuring by such resolute despatch
her present Kingdom (with a King to match).
Then why this gale of wife-forsaken sighs,
the trembling tears brushed from the brimming eyes?
What God is this, unless the God of Love,
who cannot brook his servants' long remove?
For Ptolemy, all Egypt's altars smoke
and hecatombs of bullocks loose their yoke,
while I, a ransom from a loving head,
secure a husband's swift return to bed,
who conquers Syria, the Euphrates crosses,
views India & returns with trifling losses.
Whisked hence by Venus, lo! these few hairs set
in starry payment of the royal debt.

      And yet with grief, O Queen, I left your hair,
a grief attested by your own coiffure,
by which I vow (& none vows there in vain)
no hair exists that scissors can't obtain.
Scissors & hair? Before the touch of steel
the tallest mountains have been known to reel.
Athos itself, the Guardian of the Coast,
bent to the pickaxe of the Persian host,
whereat the Thian forbears of your crown
watched a fleet passing & a mountain drown.
For women's locks what help, when such as these
yield to the metal of the Chalybes?
A plague on smithies, be they crude or fine,
cursed be the smelter, cursed the teeming mine!

      My loss was freshly mourned, when Venus sent
black Memnon's brother with Divine intent.

[164]

The winged familiar mounts; he fans the air;
he bears me upwards through the darkening sphere
until in Heaven he lays me safe at rest
in the chaste dove-cote of Cytherea's breast.
Translated thus, at Queen Arsínoe's word,
I join (though wet with tears) the golden horde.
No more shall Ariadne's Crown alone
gleam from the threshold of the Heavenly Throne:
these holy spoils (with hers) must share from now
th' immortal honours of a mortal brow.
The older stars make room. The Gods declare
th' apotheosis of a lock of hair.

Shielding the Virgin from the Lion's wrath,
(below the Bear that glisters in the North)
trampled by night upon the Milky Way
to kindly Tethys then restored by day,
westward I wheel, leading slow Boötes on
loth to sink seawards e'er the night has gone.
Unlooked-for Fate! 'Tis ill to tempt the Maid –
more abject still to leave the Truth unsaid,
or, fearful of a God's offended smart,
forbear to lend expression to the heart.
Know: less a source of gladness than of sighs
my elevation to the brilliant skies,
my heavenly lustres shine (to me) less clear
than those that hung from Berenice's ear,
who used to smooth me with sweet oils & scent
though not with myrrh, nor married ornament.

Pour then for me, upon your bridal night,
before you doff your silks & quench the light,
before your eager bosom you yield up,
the mingled fragrance of the onyx cup,

onyx, whose contents have so often led
to the chaste dalliance of the marriage bed.
Let the false tokens of unwedded lust
degraded sink into the wasteful dust.
Favoured the bride whose offerings I accept,
her husband constant, she in love adept.

    When, Berenice, you come to Venus' rites
amid the cerem'ny of palace lights,
when gazing upwards (in the cause of Love),
you fix your eyes upon the stars above,
recall the 'simple' scents I knew in life
& pour the perfumes proper to a wife.

    Let but Aquarius with Orion shine,
the stars fall inward and this Lock Divine
be placed once more on that fair head of thine!

Catullus

Sweet entrance to a husband's pleasure
      door Jove cram with goodness!
pleasant too for grandpapa's lust
      door that worked well for Balbus
while the old man was alive
      then switched fealty to madam
shutting yourself on the *ci-devant*
      face: decay possessed the old
one: they laid him out stiff & bare.
Whence this *volte-face* from husband to young wife?

Door

This, Gaius, a whitewashed door,
      is currently fee-held
of Caecilius. Envious
      onlookers indeed would
make me their whipping post & say,
"Door you are the port-hole to filthy vice".

Catullus

Your words are unconvincing: deeds
      bring words to sight & touch.

Door

How show this? Who cares?

Catullus

                Catullus.
Unlock yourself to him.

Door

Then listen. The virgin lifted
          across this threshold was
bogus, the groom not the first to
          finger her, and his short
sword hung like a strip of limp beet
          between his legs, never
cocked navelwards. And worse. Grandpa
          defiled his own son's sheets
polluting the fallen house, either
          from his own incest-blaze
or from his son's nerveless testicles.
          A steadier hand was needed
satisfactorily to unfasten . . .
to undo properly, her suspender belt.

Catullus

Egregious parent to ejac-
ulate in his son's private vulvula!

Door

There is more out of Brescia,
          overhung by Cycnean
cliffs, inthreaded by the honey-
          watered Mella, mother
of your loved Verona: there is
          gossip of an affair –
Postumius & Cornelius &
          her ill-sex with the two.

Catullus

There are people to question a
        door's knowledge of such things:
one who cannot leave the house to
        eavesdrop in the market
or step far from this lintel, swing-
        ing in & out all day.

Door

I have often caught her whispers
        with her maids rehearsing
their love-parties. I am sans ears
        sans tongue. They laugh. The same
names crop up, & a long red man's,
        whose name I bar from respect
of a disapproving eyebrow:
        there was trouble there when
he claimed cash from the family in
        respect of a reputed
impregnation of the daughter's lying belly.

68

Borne down by bitter misfortune
you send me this letter, Manlius,
blotted with tears,
            it comes like flotsam
from a spumy sea –
            from the shipwreck of your affairs –
a cry from the undertow . . .
and that you,
            whom Venus deprives
of soft sleep,
            whom the Greek Muse
no longer tempts,
            who turn restlessly
in an empty bed,
            call me 'my friend',
that you look to Catullus
            for love-gifts of Venus
& of the Holy Muses,
            is a gift in itself,
but your own tears blind you to mine.
I am not neglectful of friendship,
but we two squat in the same coracle,
we are both swamped by the same stormy waters,
I have not the gifts of a happy man. . . .
Often enough,
            when a man's toga first sat on my shoulders
I chased love & the Muses,
            in the onset of youth
the tart mixture of Venus
            seeming sweet,

but a brother's death
        drove a young man's kickshaws
into limbo –
        I have lost you, my brother
and your death has ended
        the spring season
of my happiness,
        our house is buried with you
& buried the laughter that you taught me.
There are no thoughts of love nor of poems
in my head
        since you died.
Hence, Manlius
        the reproach in your Roman letter
leaves me unmoved:
        "Why loiter in Verona,
Catullus, where
        for men of our circle
cold limbs in an empty bed
        are the rule –
not the exception?"
        Forgive me, my friend
but the dalliance of love
        that you look for
has been soured by mourning.
        As for a poem . . .
our tastes call for my Greek books,
        and those are at home
where we both live
        and where our years pile up,
in Rome . . .
        I have few copies of anything by me.

One case only has followed me North.
There is nothing curmudgeonly here –
on whom do you think
      I would sooner lavish
love-gifts of Venus
      & gifts of the Holy Muses
than you?
      You have turned to a friend
& the friend's hands are empty. . . .
How can I give what I have not got?

     ★   ★   ★   ★   ★

And yet
      lest 'Oblivion's veil'
descend
      too early on your kindness
it is right
      that the Nine Sisters
should know of my debt,
      Manlius,
they will repeat
      the words in this scroll
to unborn generations,
      your name will grow brighter
as the paper yellows,
      while the subtle spider
fails to hang
      his delicate filaments
over a neglected name.

My harrowing
      at the hands of Venus

(whom no man should ever trust)
        is well-known
in Pieria –
        how I burned like Aetnaean lava,
how I boiled like the hot springs at Thermopylae,
tears ceaselessly in my stricken eyes,
my cheeks drenched with lamentable showers,
and then, Manlius,
        as a hill stream
unexpectedly springing
        from a wind-clear crest
exchanging
        the mossed boulders
of its source
        for the steep-sloped gully
where it plunges
        precipitously
to the valley floor
        you appeared
& brought
        (with your friend's kindness)
the refreshment to me
        that the stream brings to the fissured vineyards
heavy under the hot sun
        & to the sweat-worn *contadini*
who work in them.
        You came
as the Dioscuri
        in the black-breathed storm
conjuring the right wind from the right quarter,
as Castor at the sailors' prayer,
as Pollux at the sailors' prayer.

[173]

You opened a path
        where the field had been shut before.
You gave a roof to our love,
        whose Mistress connived
at our *rencontres*
        & the love-ease that we sought there.
With supple steps
        Catullus's bright-shining Goddess
found her way thither,
        her woman's sandals
echoing
        on the worn threshold-stone.

Thus . . .
        with as flagrant desire
Laodamia
        came to Protesilaus
crossing the marriage threshold
of a house doomed to stand empty,
the blood-tribute neglected . . .
the Lords of Hill-Heaven unappeased.
Shield me,
        Rhamnusian Queen
from like joy-hastes
        by-passing Heaven
Laodamia
        learnt too well
in her swift widowing
        the thirst
of holy altars
        for their blood-due:
before the first & second winters

[174]

with their lovers' nights
      had satisfied
her bride's love-greed
& made the shattered wedding-yoke
endurable,
      her arms unclasped
her husband's neck
      who sailed for Trojan walls
and fell
      as Fate foresaw
the first to land.

For Helen's rape
      had driven Greece to arms,
Troy was the cause,
      & Troy spread death –
a common grave for the young of Asia & Achaia.
The crowds of fighting-men
      & the feats-of-arms
found their end there,
      and you, who shone in my life,
who are stretched now by the same headland . . .
I have lost you, my brother,
      your death has ended
the spring season
      of my happiness,
our house is buried with you,
& buried the laughter that you taught me.
You lie under alien ground
      among anonymous tombs
far from our reach
      far from our house-clan grave mounds:

[175]

the malign fields of the Troad cover your ashes.
There gathered
        the Argive Princes
hurriedly leaving
        home, fields & hearth
lest in an easeful bed
        Paris
unchallenged, enjoy
        the limbs of the Spartan woman
whom he had stolen.

        This was the history
of your loss
        Laodamia
who were the loveliest of the brides of Thessaly,
whose husband was sweeter to you
        than your own life
whom you loved as completely
        as the water the whirlpool,
the love-pit in your soul
        – deep as Lake Zerithon,
where Hercules hacked out the caverns under Cyllene
& drained the Stymphalian swamp of its silt waters,
when the first & the least born,
        Eurystheus,
set him to slaughter
        the man-eating cranes
which Jove's son picked-off
        with his death-bolts,
& was half-way to Heaven. . . .
        A new god

to come & go on Olympus –
      where Hebe,
the cup-bearer,
      already half-fears
for her virgin days.
      Far deeper
than such gulfs of love
      was yours, that taught
an untamed girl
      to wear
with freedom the wedlock yoke. . . .
      Love
was not more of a miracle
      for the old man with money
& an only daughter
      who, at the last minute,
produces a grandson . . .
      the family wealth
is secured,
      the child's name
inserted & witnessed in the will,
while the vulturine relatives
observed to have been perched
expectantly
      on grandpapa's grey poll
flap off
      discomfited.
No dove
      uxoriously
enjoyed its snow-white mate
with more promiscuous beak
      than you

collecting bites for kisses,
        though doves
(they say)
        are more omnivorous
than women
        when their appetites are stung.
Yet these
        beside your violence
fail,
        confronted by a fair-haired man,
Protesilaus. . . .

And the light of Catullus's own life
when she looked for his embrace
        gave little
in the matter of passion
        to you, Laodamia.
Cupid was clothed in saffron
        & shone & played
in her love-movements . . .
        who looks (it is true)
elsewhere
        for other love.
But the quests are few & secret.
I hold my tongue, remembering
that cuckolds are a tedious lot –
Juno herself
        faced with all-loving Jove's
interminable *amours*
        digests her rage. . . .
Yet men & gods make poor comparisons.

[178]

Why, like a husband, should I ape the father?
No father yielded me this daughter,
Who comes to my house
            by night
shedding Assyrian perfumes
            her husband unaware
of the love-charms that she brings me. . . .
I ask for no more,
            enough that her sweet thefts
mark white days in the calendar of my love.

      ★   ★   ★   ★   ★

Thus, Manlius,
            for the 'offices of friendship'
you have shown me,
            this gift of a poem –
not perhaps what you asked for
            but what I can do . . .
it will help
            to ward off the rust of successive years
from your name,
            & the gods will also reward you
& Themis
            who ever in the old days
kept an eye on the worthy.
            May happiness clothe you
& the woman who comforts you –
even the house of our love-games
            & its Mistress,
& he who first brought us together
the fount of so much that was good in our lives.

But beyond these
        always she
who is dearer to me than all else,
my light & my eyes
        who, living,
invests life for Catullus
        with its sweet reason.

Do not wonder when the wench declines
your thigh her thigh to place beneath.
You cannot buy them with the costliest clothes
or with extravagance of clearest stones.
There's an ugly rumour abroad,
        b.o. under the armpits –
and nobody likes that!
    So do not wonder if
a nice girl declines the goat-pit.
Either reach for the deodorant,
or cease to wonder that she so declines.

70

Lesbia says she'ld rather marry me
than anyone,
       though Jupiter himself came asking
or so she says,
       but what a woman tells her lover in desire
should be written out on air & running water.

71

If ever anyone
was deservedly plagued by a goat under his armpits
or crippled with gout,
>   your rival
who performs gratuitously on the body of your love
would appear remarkably handicapped by both complaints.
Whenever they do it, you're avenged on the pair of them:
she passes out at once under the malodour,
he's bent double in an ecstasy of gout.

72

There was a time, Lesbia, when
you confessed only to Catullus in love:
you would set me above Jupiter himself.
I loved you then
       not as men love their women
but as a father his children – his family.
To-day I know you too well
       and desire burns deeper in me
and you are more coarse
       more frivolous in my thought.
"How," you may ask, "can this be?"
Such actions as yours excite
       increased violence of love,
Lesbia, but with friendless intention.

Cancel, Catullus, the expectancies of friendship
cancel the kindnesses deemed to accrue there:
kindness is barren, friendship breeds nothing,
only the weight of past deeds growing oppressive
as Catullus has discovered, bitter & troubled,
in one he had once accounted a unique friend.

74

Gellius,
        hearing his uncle anathematise the mere mention
as well as the performance of love and love's ways
determined to take full advantage of the situation
by promptly assaulting his aunt. Uncle
was discreetly unable even to refer to the event.
Gellius could do as he wished.
                If he buggered the old man himself,
Uncle would not utter a word.

75

Reason blinded by sin, Lesbia,
a mind drowned in its own devotion:
come clothed in your excellences –
I cannot think tenderly of you,
sink to what acts you dare –
I can never cut this love.

76

If evocations of past kindness shed
ease in the mind of one of rectitude,
of bond inviolate, who never in abuse of God
led men intentionally to harm,
such, as life lasts, must in Catullus shed
effect of joy from disregarded love.
For what by man can well in act or word
be done to others has by me been done
sunk in the credit of an unregarding heart.
Why protract this pain? why not resist
yourself in mind; from this point inclining
yourself back, breaking this fallen love
counter to what the gods desire of men?
Hard suddenly to lose love of long use,
hard precondition of your sanity
regained. Possible or not, this last
conquest is for you to make, Catullus.
May the pitying gods who bring
help to the needy at the point of death
look towards me and, if my life were clean,
tear this malign pest out from my body
where, a paralysis, it creeps from limb to limb
driving all former laughter from the heart.
I do not now expect – or want – my love returned,
nor cry to the moon for Lesbia to be chaste:
only that the gods cure me of this disease
and, as I once was whole, make me now whole again.

77

Whom I have trusted to no end (Rufus)
other than expense of evil knowledge
has come to the ambush,
      inflamed viscera,
raped all that was precious.
Here was poison in rape of life
        here was disease of love.
Witness the chaste mouth of a chaste woman
soiled by loathsome saliva –
      not with impunity:
your acts shall to succeeding ages
be by the bent Sibyl broadcast, in accents of infamy.

78

Gallus's brothers possess
> one, the most attractive of wives
the other, an equally attractive son.
Gallus is a 'dear'
> arranging soft love for the lovers
putting the beautiful boy & the beautiful wife into bed
> together.
Gallus is myopic:
> himself a husband –
giving a young lad lessons in cuckoldry!

They nickname Lesbia's brother 'pulcher',
            naturally
since she prefers him to Catullus & the Catulli;
but let him dispose as he will of Catullus
            (& the Catulli)
when he finds three men of distinction
            willing to greet him in public.

80

How is it, Gellius,
      when you leave home in the morning
& again at 2 in the afternoon
      with the rest of the day before you
after your soft siesta
      that your lips
previously pink
      are unaccountably whiter than winter snow?
One is not sure,
      unless rumour speak true:
that you swallow the taut tumescence of a man's stomach.
One thing is certain
      that Virro's strained thighs
& your lips flecked with semen
      cry out in unison to onlookers.

Surely, Iuventius, one of this throng in Rome
must be more to your taste than your present guest
whose skin is the colour of old ivory
who comes from Pesaro
        a provincial backwater,
whom you've placed now in your heart,
whom you dare hold up to Catullus,
unaware of your solecism?

82

My eyes in your pledge, Quintius,
and something more precious than eyes to me;
do not touch what is more precious than my eyes,
more treasured than something more precious than pre-
    cious eyes.

Lesbia is extraordinarily vindictive
about me in front of her husband
who is thereby moved to fatuous laughter –
a man mulishly insensitive, failing to grasp
that a mindless silence (about me) spells safety
while to spit out my name in curses, baring
her white teeth, means she remembers me, and
what is more pungent still, is scratching the wound
ripening herself while she talks.

84

'*H*advantageous' breathes Arrius heavily
              when he means 'advantageous',
intending 'artificial' he labours '*h*artificial',
convinced he is speaking impeccably while
he blows his 'h's about most '*h*artificially'.
One understands that his mother – his uncle –
his family, in fact, on the distaff side
spoke so.

        Fortunately he was posted to Syria
and our ears grew accustomed to normal speech again,
unapprehensive for a while of such words
until suddenly the grotesque news reaches us
that the Ionian Sea has become
                 since the advent of Arrius
no longer Ionian
        but (inevitably) *H*ionian.

85

I hate and I love. And if you ask me how,
I do not know: I only feel it, and I'm torn in two.

86

We have heard of Quintia's beauty. To me she is tall,
    slender
and of a white 'beauty'. Such things I freely admit;
but such things do not constitute beauty.
            In her there is nothing of Venus,
not a pinch of love spice in her long body.
While Lesbia, Lesbia is loveliness indeed.
            Herself of particular beauty
has she not plundered womanhead of all its graces,
            flaunting them as her adornment?

87

No woman loved, in truth, Lesbia
as you by me;
no love-faith found so true
as mine in you.

88

What, Gellius, of the man
who itches with sister & mother
      naked in night-vigils,
who 'lies-in' for his uncle,
what stain does he lay on himself?
Such, that not Tethys to far limits
nor Ocean, father of Nereids, can cleanse:
no fouler brand (Gellius)
      even supposing
one were to lower his head to his own loins
      and swallow himself.

Gellius is thin.
                    So?
                        He possesses
an unusually agreeable mother
a similarly compliant uncle
a sister swelling with Venus
and a whole crowd of female 'connections'.
– Is he likely to put on much weight?

A taste for his sort of forbidden fruit
is no way to wax plump.

90

Let there stem (Gellius)
from the execrable conjunction of a son with his mother
a Magus skilled in Persian priestcraft, for such
if the unnatural cults of the Near East are correct
must the seed be (Gellius) of mother & son:
such only can summon the gods in song
when the grease of entrail-fat flares on the altar.

In this hopeless & wasting love of mine
I trusted you for one reason, Gellius:
not because I knew you well
        nor respected your constancy
nor thought you able (or willing) to rinse out your mind
but merely because the woman for whom
this compulsive desire is eating me
happens to be neither your mother
        nor sister
nor any other close female relative.
In spite of our intimacy I did not believe
you would find here incentive for action.
– You did,
        in the overwhelming attraction
pure sin holds for you, Gellius,
        or anything smacking of sin.

92

Lesbia loads me night & day with her curses,
'Catullus' always on her lips,
      yet I know that she loves me.
How? I equally spend myself day & night
in assiduous execration
      – knowing too well my hopeless love.

93

Utter indifference to your welfare, Caesar,
is matched only by ignorance of who you are.

94

Stuffing, O'Toole naturally stuffs with his tool:
the stew-pot stews in its own mess.

95

Nine harvests & nine winters since its inception
Cinna's *Zmyrna* is complete.
Hortalus turns out 5,000 versicles yearly.
Penetrating to the runnelled waves of Satrachus
the remote regions of its setting,

        Cinna's *Zmyrna*
shall be read by white-haired generations.
The *Annals* of Volusius will wilt by the banks of the Padua,
occasionally a limp wrapping for mackerel.
Cinna's lapidary relics are to Catullus' taste:
let the public plump for the fustian of Antimachus.

96

If, Calvus, effects of grief
        affect
those enigmatic sepulchres
        of former love
& spent friendships,
        lamented & evoked in our desire,
reflect, her early death
        will never grieve Quintilia
half so much
        as your long love must make her gay.

97

As God is my witness where is the difference between
the smell of Aemilius' mouth & that of his arse?
The cleanness of one equals the filth of the other. Actually
his arse is probably the cleaner & nicer of the two:
there he's without teeth, while the teeth in his mouth
are half a yard long, stuck in the gums like an old wagon
behind them the cleft cunt of a she-mule pissing in summer.
And this Being copulates.
                 A fit dolt for the treadmill.
Considers himself an object of elegance.
Whatever woman handles this man is equally
capable of licking the arse-hole of a leprous hangman.

98

The same can be said of you, Victius
as of any open-mouthed bore
                              suffering from halitosis.
With that tongue of yours one can actually credit
your licking, at will, besmeared boots & buttocks.
If you wish to prostrate the company –
                              gape:
you will effectively accomplish your purpose

Purloining while you played in honeyed youth
a kiss, sweeter than one suspects ambrosia tastes,
I paid, Iuventius, in full:
                              an hour or more
you racked me with my own self-exculpations
your loathing left untouched by tears.
No sooner had I kissed you
                              than with every finger
in every corner of your mouth
                              you washed & rubbed
all contact of my lips
                    like the slaver of some syphilitic whore
away. More:
            you gave me, fallen, to an enemy
                                        – Amor
who has not since ceased to rack me in his own usage,
so that a purloined kiss
                        once ambrosial,
is changed to one more acid than acid hellbane tastes.
Met with such strong despite of love
                                    my fallen love
shall from this day no kisses more purloin.

100

Undone or done up with love
Caelius for Aufilenus
          Quintius for Aufilena
that for the brother
          this for the sister
each the flower of young Verona,
something beyond 'brotherly love' . . .
which should I favour, Caelius, but you
who showed me such friendship when
the irrational flame seared me
in Rome? Be happy, Caelius. Thrive.
          Be potent in loving.

IOI

Journeying over many seas & through many countries
I come dear brother to this pitiful leave-taking
the last gestures by your graveside
the futility of words over your quiet ashes.
Life cleft us from each other
pointlessly depriving brother of brother.
Accept then, in our parents' custom
these offerings, this leave-taking
echoing for ever, brother, through a brother's tears.
                                        – 'Hail & Farewell'.

102

If, Cornelius, we entrust our secrets
only to those whom we know we can trust,
here is Catullus,
                devoted to secrets & secrecy
a finger ever to his lips,
                as mute as Harpocrates!

Either give me my hundred pounds back, Silo
and persist in your boorish, surly behaviour, or
if as a guide to tarts the money tempts you,
simply give up your boorish, surly behaviour.

104

Do you really believe I could blacken my life,
the woman dearer to me than my two eyes?
If I could
         I should not be sunk in this way in my love for her –

who performs a zoo of two-backed beasts,
daily with Tappo.

O'Toole
    attempting an entry of the *mons Parnassus*
is pitchforked by the Muses out of their (very) private
regions.

106

When an auctioneer's seen with a good-looking boy
    (by himself)
it is fair to presume that there has been purchase & sale
    – in a closed market.

107

If ever anyone anywhere, Lesbia, is looking
                        for what he knows will not happen
and then unexpectedly it happens –
                                the soul is astonished,
as we are now in each other,
                        an event dearer than gold,
for you have restored yourself, Lesbia, desired
restored yourself, longed for, unlooked for,
                                brought yourself back
to me. White day in the calendar!
                        Who happier than I?
What more can life offer
    than the longed for unlooked for event when it happens?

108

If, by general consent, it should be decided
Cominius, to cut short your reverend age
fouled by obscene habits,
      I envisage your tongue
inimical to the good
      extracted & cast to the crows,
your gouged eyeballs
      gulped down the black gullet of a raven,
entrails offal for dogs,
      your limbs to the wolves.

Joy of my life! you tell me this –
that nothing can possibly break this love of ours for each
    other.

God let her mean what she says,
                    from a candid heart,
that our two lives may be linked in their length
day to day,
      each to cach,
in a bond of sacred fidelity.

110

Men always praise an honest whore, keen
for the price of what she proposes to do,
but to promise & break promise
        frequently taking & never giving
proves the woman, Aufilena, inimical to men.
Keep either your words or your modesty intact:
perform what you offer,
        or don't make the offer at all.
To take fraudulent payment proves you
worse than the tart who avariciously
prostitutes herself with every part of her body.

III

In constancy content with one man, there
Aufilena, is the epitome of bridehood; yet
sooner your thigh put to promiscuous use
than that the one man be your uncle
and you begetting from him your own first cousins.

112

Naso! an elevated personage
with a stoop, however, bespeaking
a somewhat different sort of 'elevation'.
Indeed, an elevated person.

113

In The Year of Pompey's First Consulate, Cinna,
two men 'frequented' the First Lady,
In The Year of Pompey's Second Consulate
the same two are still at it,
but now with a cohort of others:
adultery spreads like a weed.

114

O'Toole is generally accounted
a wealthy man,
      fish fowl game
meadow & plough land,
      the broad acres near Firmum
packed with abundance.
      To what purpose?
Its owner spends more than he makes.
I salute such riches
      more apparent than real,
I praise the estate
      whose owner is lacking in substance.

115

O'Toole is the proud master of
20 acres of pasture
     & 27 acres of arable land
the rest is unfortunately swamp.
Where is our latter-day Croesus
the man loaded with such an estate,
grass plough wood moor & marsh land
stretching away to the Hyperborean North
and down to the shores of the Adriatic?
Everything here's on a grand scale
including the owner,
     and he's not a man either,
but a *tool* larger than life,
     upreared & rampant at the gates!

116

Conscientiously bringing my mind to bear on this
    problem
Gellius,
            I have thought more than once
that the example of Callimachus
            his songs sent you from me
might ease our relations
            dissuade you from bombarding me
with offensive squibs,
            all of which, I can see now,
was wasted hope & effort.
            Your darts we shall continue to parry
– with a pass of the cloak,
            while in our epigrams you stand
transfixed in ignominy.

GLOSSARY OF PROPER NAMES

Names of geographical features and/or familiar place-names which have remained constant, or nearly so, have not been included. Where necessary, substantival forms have been substituted for adjectival ones. The letter 'L', in brackets, stands for 'Lemprière', to whose eminently traditional work the reader is referred for further information.

ACHAIA. Another name for Hellas; a synonym for Greece. (Poem 68)

ACHILLES. (L.) Son of Peleus and Thetis. One of the mightiest of the Greek heroes in the Trojan War. (Poem 64)

ADONIS. (L.) A mortal youth of great beauty who was loved by Venus. (Poem 29)

AEGEUS. (L.) The father of Theseus and King of Athens. Believing his son to have been killed by the Minotaur, he threw himself into the sea, which was subsequently named the Aegean. (Poem 64)

AEMILIUS. Unidentified. (Poem 97)

AESOP. (L.) The sixth-century philosopher and fabulist who, according to tradition, lived at the court of King Croesus. (Poem 28)

AGANIPPE. One of the two springs on Mount Helicon, which were sacred to the Muses. Hippocrene was the other. (Poem 61)

ALECTO. One of the three Furies. (Poem 64)

ALFENUS. Traditionally, P. Alfenus Varus (q.v.). (Poems 10, 30)

AMASTRIS. A port near Cytorus (q.v.), and similarly situated. (Poem 4)

AMATHUSIA. Another name for Cyprus, where Venus was particularly worshipped. (Poem 36)

AMEANA. Either Mamurra's mistress, or a prostitute with whom he had dealings. Poem 41 implies she was a Cisalpine.

AMMON. (L.) The present-day oasis of Siwa in Libya. The Egyptian god Ammon was worshipped there as 'Jupiter Ammon'. (Poem 7)

AMOR. Cupid (q.v.). (Poems 45, 99)

AMPHITRITE. One of the Nereids, hence the sea. (Poem 64)

ANCON. Latin, Ancona. A town on the Adriatic coast, originally a Greek colony associated with Venus. (Poem 36)

ANDROGEOS. (L.) Son of Minos and Pasiphaë, murdered, by Aegeus, on account of his athletic prowess at the Panathenaic games. (Poem 64)

ANTIMACHUS. (L.) A sixth-century poet, author of an epic poem on the Theban War. In his own day his work was rated second only to that of Homer. (Poem 95)

ANTIUS. Unidentified; apparently involved in a law-suit in which P. Sestius was the prosecutor. (Poem 44)

AONIA. A name for Boeotia. Mount Helicon is situated there. (Poem 61)

APÁME. Berenice's mother, the wife of Magas, King of Cyrene. On her husband's death, she cancelled her daughter's engagement to Ptolemy III (246–221 B.C.), and arranged for her to marry his cousin, Demetrius, who, however, devoted his attentions to Apáme rather than Berenice, for which, under Berenice's personal direction, he was assassinated in Apáme's bedroom. Berenice subsequently married Ptolemy III. (Poem 66)

APELIOTA. The East Wind. (Poem 26)

APOLLO. (L.) Often referred to as 'Phoebus' Apollo, and thus identified with the sun, but his sphere of activity is wide. He is patron of the arts, sciences and all civilised activity. He is the son of Jupiter and Latona, and the twin of Diana. (Poem 64)

AQUINUS. A poet of the old-fashioned traditionalist school. He may be the Aquinus mentioned by Cicero in his *Tusculan Disputations* v. 63. (Poem 14)

ARGIVES. (L.) The crew of the Argo; also the inhabitants of the city of Argos, the capital of Argolis, in which sense the word is a synonym for 'Greeks'. (Poem 64)

ARIADNE. (L.) The daughter of Minos and Pasiphaë. She helped Theseus to kill the Minotaur, who was her half-brother. She and Theseus subsequently eloped; but he abandoned her on the island of Naxos. There she was consoled by Bacchus, who married her, bringing as a wedding present the Corona of seven stars, which bears her name. (Poems 64, 66)

ARRIUS. Traditionally, the self-made Q. Arrius, praetor and supporter of M. Crassus, whom he possibly accompanied to Parthia, a journey which would have entailed an Ionian crossing, such as is referred to in the poem. (Poem 84)

ARSÍNOE. (L.) Berenice's mother-in-law, the wife of Ptolemy II (283–246 B.C.). She was deified and worshipped as a manifestation of Aphrodite. (Poem 66)

ARTEMIS. Latin, Diana (L.), Apollo's twin, virgin goddess of the moon and of hunting. (Poem 64)

ASINIUS. Asinius Marrucinus, brother of C. Asinius Pollio (q.v.). (Poem 12)

ATHENE. Latin, Minerva (L.). Goddess of war and wisdom, protectress of Athens. She was said to have sprung fully armed from Jove's head. (Poem 64)

ATTIS. (L.) Archetypal devotee of the Mother Goddess. (Poem 63)

AUFILENUS/AUFILENA. Unidentified, presumably a Veronese brother and sister. (Poems 100, 110, 111)

AURELIUS. Unidentified, possibly a Cisalpine like Furius with whom he is coupled. (Poems 11, 15, 16, 21)

AURORA. (L.) The Dawn. (Poem 64)

AURUNCULEIA, Vinia (q.v.). (Poem 61)

BACCHUS. (L.) The God of wine who was the object of an ecstatic cult, similar in many respects to that of Cybele. (Poems 27, 64)

BALBUS. An unidentified Veronese. (Poem 67)

BATTIADES. A descendant of King Battus, a Spartan who built the Libyan city of Cyrene in 630 B.C., and became its first king. The term was used as a patronymic for Callimachus (q.v.). (Poem 7)

BERECYNTHIA. A mountain in Phrygia, associated with the worship of Cybele. (Poem 63)

BERENICE. (L.) Wife of Ptolemy III. Soon after her marriage her husband left for a campaign in Syria. Berenice placed a lock of her hair in her mother-in-law's shrine at Zephyrium, against his safe return. Unfortunately the lock was lost. The Royal Astronomer, Conon, was consulted, and discovered it as a new constellation, the Coma Berenices. Callimachus wrote a poem to celebrate the event. (Poems 65, 66)

BIBACULUS. M. Furius Bibaculus, a Cremonese, one of the 'new poets'.

BITHYNIA. A Roman province on the south-western shores of the Black Sea. (Poems 10, 25, 31)

BOÖTES. The constellation of Arcturus. (Poem 66)

CAECILIUS. Unidentified, presumably a Cisalpine. The name appears in poems 35 and 67, and may or may not refer to the same person.

CAELIUS. M. Caelius Rufus (*q.v.*). (Poems 58, 100)

CAESAR. (L.) C. Julius Caesar, the dictator; the object of some of Catullus's most virulent epigrams in which the poet ridicules his reputed pederasty and his patronage of Mamurra. (Poems 11, 54, 57, 93)

CAESIUS. An unidentified poet but, like Aquinus, with whom he is linked, evidently a follower of the traditionalist school. (Poem 14)

CALLIMACHUS. (L.) The Greek poet, a native of Cyrene (died 250 B.C.). He lived at Alexandria where he worked in the Library. He was especially admired by the poets of Catullus's circle and wrote the elegant piece of court poetry of which poem 66 is a direct translation. (Poems 65, 116)

CALVUS. C. Licinius Calvus, poet and orator; a close friend of Catullus and a colleague of Cicero. As a writer he is linked by Ovid with Catullus and Tibullus. He was probably a small man, *vide* the last line of poem 53. (Poems 14, 50, 53, 96)

CAMERIUS. Unidentified. (Poem 55)

CASTOR. (L.) One of the Dioscuri (*q.v.*). (Poems 4, 68)

CATO. Almost certainly P. Valerius Cato, a Veronese freedman, born *c.*100 B.C., poet and man of letters. His influence on his younger contemporaries appears to have been great. He may well have been the original source of the new movement in poetry. (Poem 56)

CATULLUS. C. Valerius Catullus (*c.* 84 – *c.* 54 B.C.), a Veronese who lived in Rome and was one of the principal figures of the new school of poetry referred to disparagingly by Cicero as 'the moderns'. They sought to apply Alexandrian criticism and technique to Latin poetry. Catullus is known to have visited Asia Minor for a year, and to have lost a brother in the same part of the world. He was a member of Clodia's circle, and was accepted by her as one of her lovers. (Poems 2, 6, 7, 8, 9, 12, 14, 15, 21, 28, 30, 31, 35, 40, 42, 44, 46, 49, 51, 52, 55, 56, 58, 63, 67, 68, 72, 73, 76, 79, 81, 92, 95, 102)

CHALYBES. (L.) The inhabitants of a region in Asia Minor, near Pontus which was celebrated for its iron mines. (Poem 66)

CHIRON. (L.) The Centaur, Peleus's grandfather and the future tutor of Achilles. He lived on the slopes of Mount Pelion. (Poem 64)

CICERO. (L.) M. Tullius Cicero, the orator, statesman and author. His year as consul coincided with the Cataline conspiracy. He incurred the enmity of Caesar's faction and was driven into exile by P. Clodius Pulcher. His speech *Pro Caelio*, defending M. Caelius Rufus, provides us with the only full-length portrait of Clodia. Although he was an intimate of many of Catullus's friends, poem 49 is the only direct link between the two to have been preserved.

CIEROS. A town in Thessaly. (Poem 64)

CINNA. C. Helvius Cinna, a Cisalpine and friend of Catullus; one of the 'new poets'. He probably accompanied Catullus, under the patronage of C. Memmius, to Bithynia. He was murdered in the confusion after Caesar's death in mistake for Cinna the conspirator, as in Shakespeare's play. (Poems 10, 95, 113)

CLIVUS VICTORIAE. The exclusive residential street on the Palatine, where Clodia and her brother lived. (Poem 37)

CLODIA. (L.) Clodia Metelli, the wife of Q. Metellus Celer, her cousin. She was reputed to have innumerable lovers and, on her husband's death, was suspected of having poisoned him. Much of Catullus's most vitriolic as well as some of his tenderest poetry was inspired by her.

CNIDOS. A city in Caria in which there were three temples dedicated to Venus. (Poem 36)

COLCHIS. (L.) A region at the far end of the Black Sea. The Argonauts sailed to Colchis, to obtain the Golden Fleece. (Poem 64)

COLOGNA VENETA. A small town near Verona. There used to be a bridge there called *Il Ponte di Catullo*. (Poem 17)

COLOSSUS. (L.) An immense bronze statue a hundred and five feet high, straddling the entrance to the harbour of Rhodes. It was known as one of the wonders of the world. (Poem 4)

COMINIUS. Unidentified. (Poem 108)

CORNELIUS. Cornelius Nepos (*q.v.*). (Poems 1, 67, 102)

CORNIFICIUS. Q. Cornificius, the quaestor (48 B.C.), who espoused the Senatorial cause and was killed in battle in 41. He was one of the 'new poets', a friend of Catullus and Cicero. (Poem 38)

CRANNON. One of the principal towns of Thessaly. (Poem 64)

[233]

CROESUS. (L.) The fabulously rich king of Lydia. (Poem 115)

CUPID. (L.) The son of Venus, traditionally armed with bow and arrows, who inspires the victims of his archery with erotic passion. In the plural, 'the spirits of love'. (Poems 3, 13, 36, 64, 68)

CYBEBE. Another name for Cybele (*q.v.*). In poem 63, Catullus uses both forms, the first 'e' of 'Cybebe' being long, and that of 'Cybele' short.

CYBELE. (L.) The Mother Goddess. Her cult, which was ecstatic, was of Phrygian origin. It reached Greece in the sixth century B.C., and was introduced into Rome in the Second Punic War. Her temple stood on the Palatine, behind Clodia's house. (Poem 35)

CYCLADES. A group of islands in the Aegean. (Poem 4)

CYCNEA. An old fortress dominating Brescia. (Poem 67)

CYLLENE. A mountain in Arcadia on whose slopes there was a town of the same name. (Poem 68)

CYNTHIA. Another name for Diana (*q.v.*). (Poem 66)

CYTHEREA. (L.) The adjectival form of 'Cythera', the modern Cerigo, an island off the coast of Laconia. According to some authorities, it was the scene of Venus's emergence from the sea. Hence, she was often called 'Cytherea'. (Poem 66)

CYTORUS. A port in Paphlagonia on the borders of Bithynia. It lay at the foot of a mountain of the same name, famous for its box-wood. (Poem 4)

DARDANIA. Another name for the Troad (*q.v.*). (Poem 65)

DELOS. An island in the Cyclades, holy to Diana, who was said to have been born there. (Poem 34)

DELPHOS. (L.) A city in Phocis, said to be situated at the centre of the earth. Its Bacchantes, or female worshippers of Bacchus, were called 'Thyiades'. (Poem 64)

DIANA. (L.) Virgin goddess of the moon and of hunting. (Poem 34)

DINDYMIA. A mountain in Phrygia, associated with Cybele. Hence, another name for the goddess. (Poem 63)

DIOSCURI. Castor and Pollux, twin sons of Jupiter, who protect sailors in times of storm. They constitute the zodiacal sign of Gemini. (Poems 4, 57, 68)

EGNATIUS. Unidentified. (Poems 37, 39)

EMATHIA. Another name for Thessaly, birthplace of Achilles. (Poem 64)

ENDYMION. A mortal youth loved by Diana. In order to keep him to herself she confined him to a cave on Mount Latmos and condemned him to a state of perpetual sleep. (Poem 66)

EPIDAMNUS. The Roman Dyrrachium, modern Durres, a busy crossing-place on the Adriatic. A thriving port would indicate a thriving cult of Venus, hence the reference in poem 36.

ERINYES. (L.) The three Furies. They hound those who disregard natural law, whether intentionally or otherwise. (Poem 64)

ERIUS. An unidentified intimate of Caesar. (Poem 54)

ERYX. A mountain on the west coast of Sicily, where there was a temple dedicated to Venus. (Poem 64)

EUROPA. (L.) The mother, by Jove, of Minos King of Crete. The god appeared to her in the shape of a bull, carried her to Crete and secured her there under the guardianship of the bronze giant, Talus. (Poem 55)

EUROTAS. A river in Laconia, not far from Sparta. (Poem 64)

EURYSTHEUS. (L.) The cousin of Hercules, who was subject to him. It was Eurystheus who ordered Hercules to perform his twelve labours. (Poem 68)

EUXINE LAKE. The Black Sea. (Poem 64)

FABULLUS. Unidentified. He apparently served in Spain, and possibly in Macedonia, in the same sort of capacity as Catullus in Bithynia. He is coupled with Veranius. (Poems 12, 13, 28, 47)

FALERNIAN. A type of wine. (Poem 27)

FIRMUM. A town in Picenum, near which Mamurra had an estate. (Poem 114)

FLAVIUS. Unidentified. (Poem 6)

FORMIANUS. Mamurra (*q.v.*). (Poems 41, 43)

FURIUS. Probably M. Furius Bibaculus (*q.v.*). (Poems 11, 16, 23, 24, 26)

GAIUS. Catullus. (Poem 67)

GALLAE. (L.) The priests of Cybele, so called from the river Gallus in Phrygia, whose waters maddened those who drank from it.

The Gallae, as a final service to the goddess, castrated themselves during her rite, hence the dramatic change of sex in the poem. (Poem 63)

GALLUS. Unidentified. (Poem 78)

GELLIUS. L. Gellius Poplicola (*q.v.*). (Poems 74, 80, 88, 89, 90, 91, 116)

GOLGOS. Golgi, a town in Cyprus, associated with Venus. (Poems 36, 64)

GUA. The river at Cologna Veneta, once spanned by the *Ponte di Catullo*. (Poem 17)

HAMADRYADS. Tree nymphs, whose life is the physical life of the tree. (Poem 61)

HARPOCRATES. (L.) Horus, the Egyptian child-god of silence. (Poem 102)

HEBE. (L.) Goddess of eternal youth, who was conceived by Juno as the result of a diet of lettuces. She became Hercules's wife after his apotheosis. (Poem 68)

HECAT. (L.) Also called Trivia, since her presence is particularly felt where three roads met. She represents the moon on the wane and, as such, is one of the aspects of Diana. She conducts the souls of dead women to Hades. (Poem 34)

HELEN. (L.) The most beautiful woman in the world, the wife of Menelaus King of Sparta. Her abduction by Paris was the immediate cause of the Trojan War. (Poem 68)

HELICON. A mountain in Boeotia, the home of the Muses and of Hymen. (Poem 61)

HERCULES. (L.) Jove's son by Alcmena. He was the greatest of mortal heroes, celebrated for his twelve labours and subsequent apotheosis. He was also one of the Argonauts. (Poems 55, 68)

HORTALUS (L.) Q. Hortensius Hortalus, praetor and consul, died 50 B.C., a distinguished lawyer and friend of Cicero. Although one of the 'new poets' and the recipient of poems 65 and 66, his verse does not appear to have met with Catullus's approval: *vide* poem 95.

HYMEN. (L.) Also Hymenaeus. The god of marriage, who lives on Mount Helicon in the company of the Muses. (Poems 61, 62, 64)

HYPERBOREI. (L.) A race who lived beyond the region where the North Wind starts to blow, said to be in Thrace. (Poem 115)

HYRCANIA. A wild and desolate country of Asia. (Poem 11)

IDA. (L.) A mountain in the Troad, which was originally part of Phrygia (poem 63), and also (poem 64), a mountain in Crete.

IDALIA. A district in Cyprus where there was a grove sacred to Venus. (Poems 36, 64)

IPSÍTHILLA. Unidentified. From the poem (32), almost certainly not a prostitute in our sense, but more likely a hetæra, or a freed-woman, whom Catullus knew.

ITYLUS. The Homeric name for Itys (L.), son of Tereus and Procne (*q.v.*). He was killed by his mother, who gave him to his father to eat after she had learnt that Tereus had violated her sister. (Poem 65)

IUVENTIUS. Unidentified. (Poems 24, 48, 81, 99)

JOVE. Jupiter (*q.v.*). (Poems 7, 64, 67, 68)

JUNO. (L.) Queen of Heaven, Jove's wife and sister. (Poems 64, 68)

JUNO LUCINA. Patron of childbirth, an aspect of Diana* (L.). (Poem 34)

JUPITER. (L.) The father of the gods, and lord of the upper regions, as his two brothers, Neptune and Pluto, are of the sea and the underworld respectively. Neptune was believed to have built the walls of Troy. (Poems 70, 72)

LADAS. One of Alexander the Great's couriers, who ran so swiftly that he left no footprints. (Poem 55)

LAMPSACUS. (L.) A town near the Dardanelles, noted for its oysters and its devotion to Priapus. (Poem 18)

LANUVIUM. A town in Latium. (Poem 39)

LAODAMIA. (L.) The wife of Protesilaus. She was so distressed by the loss of her husband, which occurred almost immediately after their marriage, that she had a life-size statue made of him, which she kept concealed in her bed, and with which she practised a form of hierogamy. When her father heard of this, he ordered the

---

* It is a tenable theory that many of the goddesses of Greek mythology represent the fragmentation of a pre-Greek female figure in whose person their various functions were originally met.

statue to be burnt; but Laodamia proved her loyalty by immolating herself with it. (Poem 68)

LARISSA. A town in Thessaly on the River Peneus. (Poem 64)

LATIUM. A region of Italy. (Poem 57)

LATMOS. A mountain in Caria where Endymion was kept asleep by Diana. (Poem 66)

LATONA. (L.) The mother, by Jupiter, of Diana, to whom she gave birth leaning against an olive tree in Delos. (Poem 34)

LAVINIA. Vinia (*q.v.*).

LESBIA. Clodia Metelli (*q.v.*). (Poems 2, 3, 5, 7, 8, 11, 36, 43, 51, 58, 70, 72, 75, 76, 79, 83, 86, 87, 92, 107)

LIBO. An unidentified intimate of Caesar. (Poem 54)

LUCIFER. The light-bringer, the name by which Hesperus, the evening star, is known in the morning. (Poem 62)

MAENAD. A Bacchante, or female devotee of Bacchus; the term was also applied to the worshippers of Cybele. (Poems 63, 64)

MAGUS. A wise man or magician, particularly in reference to the Persians. (Poem 90)

MAMURRA. (L.) Caesar's chief engineer in Gaul, one of the dictator's intimates. He came from Formia in Latium. Hence, Catullus sometimes calls him 'Formianus'. (Poems 29, 57)

MANLIUS. L. Manlius Torquatus (*q.v.*). (Poems 61, 68)

MARCUS TULLIUS. (L.) Marcus Tullius Cicero (*q.v.*). (Poem 49)

MARS. (L.) The god of war, whom Vulcan, the lame blacksmith god, trapped under a net of fine-spun steel, while Mars was enjoying Vulcan's wife, Venus. (Poems, 17, 64)

MEGAERA. One of the three Furies (Poem 64)

MELLA. A river near Brescia. (Poem 67)

MEMMIUS. (L.) C. Memmius Gemellus, praetor in 58 B.C., governor of Bithynia in 57; a patron of Catullus whom he took with him to Bithynia. He was himself a poet of the new school. (Poems 10, 28)

MEMNON. King of Ethiopia, one of the sons of Aurora, the dawn. (Poem 66)

MENENIUS. Unidentified. (Poem 59)

MIDAS. (L.) The Phrygian King who turned all that he touched to gold. (Poem 24)

MINOA. A town in Crete. 'Minoan' is a synonym for 'Cretan', after Minos (L.), the first king. (Poem 64)

NASO. Unidentified. (Poem 112)

NAXOS. (L.) The largest of the Cyclades, where Bacchus was held in particular honour. It was the scene of Theseus's desertion of Ariadne and of her subsequent consolation by Bacchus. (Poem 64)

NEPOS. (L.) Cornelius Nepos, the historian, a friend of Cicero, possibly a Veronese. The *Carmina*, as we have it, is dedicated to him. It is not known whether all the references to 'Cornelius' are to the same person.

NEREIDS. (L.) The Nymphs of the Aegean sea. (Poems 64, 88)

NICAEA. A town in Bithynia. (Poem 46)

NONNIUS. Identification is uncertain, but we know that the curule aedileship for 54 B.C. was awarded to M. Nonnius Sufenas of Pompey's faction. (Poem 52)

OCEAN. (L.) Oceanus, the river-god, husband of Tethys; his waters girdled the earth. (Poems 64, 88)

OLYMPUS. (L.) The home of the gods. A mountain on the borders of Macedonia and Thessaly. (Poems 34, 64, 68)

ORCUS. Pluto, the god of the dead; hence, one of the names for the underworld. (Poem 3)

OREADS. The nymphs of caves and of mountains. (Poem 64)

O'TOOLE. Mamurra (*q.v.*). (Poems 94, 105, 114, 115)

OTTO. An unidentified intimate of Caesar. (Poem 54)

PANATHANAEA. (L.) The yearly sports held at Athens in honour of Athene. (Poem 64)

PARCAE. (L.) The three Fates, who weave the web of man's destiny. (Poem 64)

PARIS. (L.) One of the sons of Priam King of Troy, celebrated for his good looks. His elopement with Helen caused the Trojan War. (Poems 61, 68)

PARNASSUS. (L.) A mountain in Phocis sacred to Apollo and the Muses. (Poems 64, 105)

PARTHIA. A country in Asia, famous for its mounted archers. (Poem 11)

PASITHEA. One of the Graces, betrothed to the god of sleep. (Poem 63)

PEGASUS. (L.) The winged horse who, by stamping with his hoof, created the spring of Hippocrene on Mount Helicon. Hence, he represents the act of poetic creation. (Poem 55)

PELEUS. One of the Argonauts, King of Thessaly and grandson of Chiron the centaur. He was the only mortal to be awarded a goddess, Thetis, for a wife. (Poem 64)

PELION. (L.) A mountain in Thessaly. (Poem 64)

PENELOPE. (L.) Wife of Odysseus. She waited faithfully for twenty years for his return from Troy. (Poem 61)

PENEUS. (L.) A river in Thessaly. (Poem 64)

PERSEUS. (L.) The son of Jupiter and Danae. The winged sandals of Mercury were one of the gifts which the gods gave Perseus so that he could kill the Gorgon, Medusa. (Poem 55)

PESARO. A town on the Adriatic, in the Roman region of Umbria. It was low-lying and unhealthy. (Poem 81)

PHAETON. (L.) The son of Apollo. He was loved by Venus, a fact which made him so conceited that he tried to drive his father's chariot, but perished in the attempt. He fell to earth, landing in the River Po, since when his three sisters, Lampetrie, Phaetusa and Lampethusa, who are known as the Heliads, and are, in reality, the poplars which line the river banks, weep tears of amber for their lost brother. (Poem 64)

PHARSALIA. A plain in Thessaly named after the town of Pharsalus. (Poem 64)

PHRYGIA. (L.) A country in Asia Minor, noted for the worship of Cybele. (Poems 46, 63, 64)

PHTHIOTIC TEMPE. (L.) A beautiful valley in Thessaly situated between Olympus and Ossa. It is watered by the River Peneus. (Poem 64)

PIERIA. Traditionally regarded as the home of poetry. It was a district on the borders of Thessaly and Macedonia. (Poems 65, 68)

PIRAEUS. The harbour about three miles outside Athens. (Poem 64)

PISO. Traditionally, L. Calpurnius Piso Caesoninus, Caesar's father-in-law. (Poems 28, 47)

POLLIO. (L.) 'Pollionus' in the English translation. C. Asinius Pollio,

Supporter of Caesar and subsequently of the Triumvirate. He was a distinguished orator, patron and poet. (Poem 12)

POLLUX. (L.) One of the Dioscuri (*q.v.*). (Poems 4, 68)

POLYXENA. (L.) One of Priam's daughters. After the fall of Troy, she was sacrificed by Neoptolemus on his father's (Achilles's) tomb. (Poem 64)

POMPEY. (L.) Cn. Pompeius Magnus, contender with Julius Caesar for sole supremacy of the Roman world (poem 113). The battle of Pharsalia (48 B.C.) decided the issue in Caesar's favour. In 55 B.C. he opened a new *piazza* in the Campus Martius. This fact helps to date poem 55.

PONTIC SEA. The Black Sea. (Poems 4, 29)

POPLICOLA. L. Gellius Poplicola, presumably a rival for Clodia's favours. Later, in 36 B.C., he became consul. He fought for Antony at Actium.

PORCIUS. Unidentified. (Poem 47)

POSTUMIA. Unidentified. It was customary for a male member of a party to preside over the toasts, etc., but for a female most unusual, and suggests licentiousness. (Poem 27)

POSTUMIUS. Unidentified, presumably a Cisalpine. (Poem 67)

PRIAPUS. (L.) The god of gardens and of lust, the most prominent feature of whose statues was a disproportionately large phallus. (Poems 18, 47)

PROCNE. (L.) The wife of Tereus, King of Thrace. When her husband discovered the fate of their son, Itylus (*q.v.*), he tried to kill her, but the gods saved her by turning her into a swallow. (Poem 65)

PROMETHEUS. (L.) The Titan who stole fire – free will – from Heaven and gave it to mankind. Jupiter punished him by chaining him for thirty years to a rock in the Caucasus. Every day an eagle devoured his liver, and every night Jove provided him with a new one. He was finally released by Hercules. (Poem 64)

PROTESILAUS. (L.) The husband of Laodamia. It had been foretold that the first Greek to land at Troy would be killed as soon as he set foot on the beach. Protesilaus knew this, but was nevertheless the first to jump from the boats. (Poem 68)

PTOLEMY III. (L.) (246–221 B.C.), husband of Berenice. The two were cousins, the relationship of brother and sister, referred to in the text, being an erotic honorific, customary in ancient Egypt. (Poem 66)

PULCHER. P. Clodius Pulcher, a notorious associate of Caesar. He succeeded in driving Cicero abroad and then pillaging his house and goods. He profaned the Mysteries of the Mother Goddess by attending them dressed as a woman. He was also said to have committed incest with his sisters. (See in Lemprière under 'Clodius'.) (Poem 79)

QUINTIA. Unidentified. (Poem 86)

QUINTILIA. Either the wife, the mistress or the betrothed of C. Licinius Calvus. (Poem 96)

QUINTIUS. Unidentified. (Poems 82, 100)

RAVIDUS. Unidentified; a rival for Clodia's favours. (Poem 40)

RHAMNUSIA. Another name for Nemesis or Fate. (Poem 68)

RHESUS. (L.) The King of Thrace whose horses were renowned for their speed. (Poem 55)

RIVER OF PHEASANTS. Phasis, a river in Colchis that rises in the Caucasus and empties into the Black Sea. It was the home of our European pheasants. (Poem 64)

RUFULUS. Unidentified. (Poem 59)

RUFUS. (L.) M. Caelius Rufus, a disciple of Cicero, who defended him against Clodius Pulcher's charges of involvement in the Cataline conspiracy. He was one of Clodia's lovers, but had broken with her by the time of the trial. As he is not known to have come from Cisalpine Gaul the Caelius of poem 100 cannot be referred to him with any certainty. (Poem 77)

SABINE. The Sabini were a neighbouring people who lived between the Nar and the Anio and were ultimately subdued by the Romans. The region near Tibur still preserved their name, but, unlike Tibur, did not provide a fashionable address. (Poems 39, 44)

SACIA. A country in Asia, bordering on the Caspian Sea. (Poem 11)

SAPPHO. (L.) The seventh-century Greek lyric poet (poem 35). Poem 51 is a direct translation of one of her poems. It marks the first known use of the Sapphic metre in Latin.

SATRACHUS. A city and river in Cyprus. (Poem 95)

SATURNALIA. (L.) The midwinter feast of Saturn. People gave each other presents; the shops closed, and an air of licence and merry-making prevailed. (Poem 14)

SATYRS. (L.) Demi-gods with the legs, hooves and horns of goats, who attended on Bacchus. (Poem 64)

SCAMANDER. (L.) One of the principal rivers of the Troad. (Poem 64)

SCYLLA. A twelve-necked monster on the Italian side of the Straits of Messina, opposite Charybdis, the whirlpool. (Poem 60)

SERAP. An Egyptian divinity whose temple stood in the suburbs of Rome. Serapis was identified by Apollodorus with the bull Apis, before whom women used to display themselves as a cure for sterility, and with whose priests they would, for similar purposes, have intercourse. The cult was ratified by Antoninus Pius in 146 A.D., but got out of hand and had to be suppressed. (Poem 10)

SESTIUS. P. Sestius, quaestor in 63 B.C., a close friend and colleague of Cicero. (Poem 44)

SIBYL. (L.) A prophetess of Apollo. The books of the most cele-brated, the Cumaean Sibyl, were preserved on the Capitol. (Poem 77)

SILENES. (L.) Another word for Satyrs, and fauns generally. Silenus was a demi-god, Bacchus's principal attendant. (Poem 64)

SILO. Unidentified. (Poem 103)

SIMONIDES. (L.) The Greek lyric poet (556–467 B.C.). (Poem 38)

SIRMIO. The promontory on Lago di Garda where Catullus, or his father, owned a villa. (Poem 31)

SOCRATION. Unidentified. (Poem 47)

SPARTA. (L.) The capital of Laconia. Helen was the Queen of Sparta.

STYMPHALIA. From Stymphalus the name of a mountain, a town and a lake in Arcadia. It was the scene of Hercules's sixth labour, the slaughter of the man-eating stymphalides, monstrous birds who lived on an island in the lake. (Poem 68)

STYX. (L.) One of the rivers of the underworld. (Poem 65)

SUFFENUS. Unidentified, evidently a poet of the traditionalist school. (Poems 14, 22)

SUFFICIO. Unidentified intimate of Caesar. (Poem 54)

SULLA. Unidentified. (Poem 14)

SYRTES. (L.) Shoal water off the North African coast. (Poem 64)

TALASIUS. (L.) The Latin name for Hymen. (Poem 61)

TAPPO. Unidentified. (Poem 104)

TAURUS. A mountain in Asia Minor. (Poem 64)

TELEMACHUS. (L.) The son of Odysseus and Penelope. (Poem 61)

TETHYS. (L.) Sea goddess, wife of Oceanus. (Poems 64, 66, 88)

THALLUS. Unidentified. (Poem 25)

THEMIS. (L.) The goddess of Justice, traditionally depicted with scales and sword. She was the mother of the Parcae. (Poem 68)

THESEUS. (L.) Son of Aegeus King of Athens. He was brought up in Troezene. He sailed to Crete and slew the Minotaur, subsequently eloping with Ariadne whom he abandoned on Naxos – some say in favour of her sister, Phaedra. (Poem 64)

THESPIA. A town in Boeotia, near Mount Helicon. (Poem 61)

THETIS. (L.) A Nereid, wife of Peleus, by whom she bore Achilles. (Poem 64)

THIA. Another name for Macedonia. The Macedonians supported Xerxes' invasion of Greece, and the Ptolemaic dynasty, to whom the word is applied, were of Macedonian origin. (Poem 66)

THYIADES. Another name for Maenads, or Bacchantes, but especially applied to those of Delphos. (Poem 64)

THYNIA. A town in Bithynia. (Poem 31)

TIBUR. Modern Tivoli, a town on the Anio near Rome. It provided a fashionable country-address. (Poems 39, 44)

TISIPHONE. One of the three Furies. (Poem 64)

TORQUATUS. L. Manlius Torquatus, an orator and friend of Cicero. He was a supporter of Pompey; quaestor in 49 B.C.; killed in the Civil War, in North Africa in 47. (Poems 61, 68)

TROAD. The region round Troy. (Poem 68)

TROEZENE. A town in Argolis. Theseus was born and brought up there. (Poem 64)

TROY. A town near the Dardanelles. The scene of the Trojan War, which in Catullus symbolises the close of the age of the gods. (Poems 64, 68)

URANIA. (L.) One of the Muses, patron of astronomy. (Poem 61)

VARUS. P. Alfenus Varus, a Cremonese mentioned by Horace in his first satire as having given up a cobbler's shop for a career in the law courts. He was the first Cisalpine to attain the consulate. (Poems 10, 22)

VATINIUS. (L.) P. Vatinius, quaestor in 63 B.C., tribune in 59, praetor in 55 and consul in 47. He was a supporter of Caesar and a friend of Cicero. He was involved in several court cases in more than one of which Licinius Calvus was the prosecutor. On one occasion, when the case was going against him, Clodius and his henchmen forcibly broke up the proceedings. (Poems 14, 52, 53)

VENUS. (L.) Born of sea-foam. The wife of Vulcan, Mars's mistress, Cupid's mother. She is the goddess of elemental attraction. (Poems 3, 13, 29, 36, 45, 56, 61, 64, 66, 68, 86, 89)

VERANIUS. Also 'Veraniolus' in the English translation. Like Fabullus (q.v.), a close friend of Catullus. (Poems 12, 28, 47)

VESPER. Another name for Hesperus, or the planet Venus, which, in common with the moon, the sun and the other stars, was thought of as rising behind Mount Oeta in Thessaly. (Poem 62)

VIBENNIUS. Unidentified. (Poem 33)

VICTIUS. Unidentified. (Poem 98)

VINIA. The wife of L. Manlius Torquatus. Otherwise unidentified. (Poem 61)

VIRRO. Unidentified. (Poem 80)

VOLUSIUS. Unidentified. A long-winded poet, presumably contemporary with Catullus. (Poems 36, 95)

VULCAN (L.) The blacksmith god who married Venus. When he was born, his mother, Juno, threw him out of Heaven because he was so ugly. As a result, he broke his leg and has remained lame ever afterwards. At Jupiter's behest he made the first woman on earth, Pandora. He is celebrated for being the only person successfully to make a mockery of Love and War, heavy armour precluding the performance of one and rendering impotent the effects of the other. (Poem 36)

ZEPHYRUS. (L.) The West Wind, brother of Memnon, one of the sons of Aurora, the Dawn. (Poems 26, 46, 64)

ZERITHON. The local name for Pheneus, a town in Arcadia, with a lake of the same name. (Poem 68)

ZMYRNA. The title of a poem by C. Helvius Cinna, probably a miniature epic like the *Peleus and Thetis*. (Poem 95)

MORE ABOUT PENGUINS
AND PELICANS

OVID

METAMORPHOSES

Translated by Mary M. Innes

Ovid (43 B.C.–A.D. 17) was among the most sophisticated of Latin writers, yet he was also a prince of storytellers, and his *Metamorphoses*, a poem in fifteen books, is a fresh, charming collection of tales. These he culled from Greek poems and myths, Latin folk-lore, and even from Babylon and the East. The unity of theme is that of transformation: of chaos changed into harmony, of animals turned into stone, of men and women who became trees or stars. The whole of western European literature has derived inspiration from the *Metamorphoses*, which are translated here by Mary M. Innes.

VIRGIL

THE PASTORAL POEMS

Translated by E. V. Rieu

Virgil (70–19 B.C.), though a shy and retiring thinker and philosopher, was the poet most esteemed at court in the early days of the Roman Empire. His pastoral poems, the *Eclogues*, were the first which Virgil published in book form and established his reputation. They reveal the Arcadian world of Virgil's memories and fancy and his perception of the realities that underlie our relation to the world around us. At times serious, they are always enchanting and provide a perfect introduction to the delights of Latin poetry. This edition includes the Latin text and ten explanatory essays.

Also published

THE AENEID

LUCRETIUS

ON THE NATURE OF THE UNIVERSE

Translated by Ronald Latham

Lucretius (*c.* 100–*c.* 55 B.C.), who devoted his life to the exposition of the teachings of Epicurus, wrote with the force of an unshakeable personal conviction in the material-istic doctrine. This poet's view of the scientific attitude of his time towards matter, atoms, the workings of the mind, cosmology, and geology, *inter alia*, can be read today as it was intended two thousand years ago: as an appeal to a disillusioned age to take comfort from the sanity of science.

R. E. Latham's direct and lucid prose translation makes clear for the reader both the differences and the resemblances between ancient and modern materialism.

THE ODYSSEY

HOMER

Translated by E. V. Rieu

Homer's *Odyssey*, composed some three thousand years ago, is still among the very pinnacles of all literature. The story of Odysseus' epic voyage home from Troy to his kingdom of Ithaca brims, like some splendid novel, with a fathomless humanity.

In his introduction to this famous edition Dr Rieu states: 'I have done my best to make Homer easy reading for those who are unfamiliar with the Greek world.' This is too modest. His inspired translations of *The Odyssey* and *The Iliad* have made Homer a modern best-seller.

THE ODES OF HORACE

Translated by James Michie

The verses of Horace (65–8 B.C.) move with the grace and inevitability of proverbs: few poets have ever been so readily quoted. His tolerant humanity, his sane belief in the golden mean, and his melancholy recognition of life's brevity have invested him, in the minds of thousands of Europeans, with the quality of a friend. The Latin text of Horace's odes on love and friendship and wine, on Roman greatness and the character of the ideal citizen, appears in this edition opposite modern translations which vary their metres to suit the lyrical forms of the original.

PETRONIUS

THE SATYRICON AND THE FRAGMENTS

Translated by John Sullivan

Translations of *The Satyricon* have in the past tended to
appear in limited editions and discreet bindings. Serious
critics, however, have regarded these racy adventures of
the ill-starred Encolpius sometimes as satire, sometimes as
a picaresque odyssey, and even as the first realistic novel in
European literature. The work, of which only a small part
survives, was almost certainly composed in the middle of
the first century A.D. by one of Nero's favourites. In form
it is extremely loose, and witty anecdotes, poetry, and dis-
course on literature and art constantly interrupt the entertaining chain of sexual and prandial orgies.

JUVENAL

THE SIXTEEN SATIRES

Translated by Peter Green

The splendour, squalor, and complexity of the Roman scene were never more vividly presented than by the satirist Juvenal (*c.* A.D. 55–130). His bitter and forcible verses were written during the reigns of Trajan and Hadrian, which Gibbon (from a safe distance) called 'the period in the history of the world during which the condition of the human race was most happy and prosperous'. To quote Peter Green's introduction, 'Juvenal does not work out a coherent ethical critique of institutions or individuals: he simply hangs a series of moral portraits on the wall and forces us to look at them.'

THE PENGUIN CLASSICS

Some Recent and Forthcoming Volumes

Livy
ROME AND THE MEDITERRANEAN
*Translated by Henry Bettenson with an
introduction by A. H. MacDonald*

Flaubert
BOUVARD AND PÉCUCHET
Translated by A. J. Krailsheimer

LIVES OF THE LATER CAESARS
Translated by Anthony Birley

Aretino
SELECTED LETTERS
Translated by George Bull

THE MABINOGION
Translated by Jeffrey Gantz

Balzac
URSULE MIROUËT
Translated by Donald Adamson

EGIL'S SAGA
Translated by Hermann Pálsson and Paul Edwards

THE PSALMS
Translated by Peter Levi

De Chinese Horoscoop

AAP

Kwok Man-ho

B

BOSCH & KEUNING

EEN DORLING KINDERSLEY BOEK

Aan de oorspronkelijke editie werkten mee:
Sharon Lucas (senior editor), Camilla Fox (art editor), Krystyna Mayer (managing editor), Derek
Coombes (managing art director), Doug Miller (DTP designer), Antony Heller (production controller).

Artwork: Danuta Mayer 4, 8, 11, 17, 27, 29, 31, 33, 35; Giuliano Fornari 21; Jane Thomson;
Sarah Ponder.

Speciale fotografie van Steve Gorton. Ook dank aan het Bristol City Museum & Art Gallery,
oriëntaalse afdeling; het British Museum, Chinese Post Office, het Powell-Cotton Museum, en de
beheerders van het Victoria & Albert Museum.

Aanvullende fotografie: Eric Crichton, Jo Foord, Philip Gatward, Steve Gorton, Dave King, Stephen
Oliver, Tim Ridley, Matthew Ward.

Fotoverantwoording: Circa Photo Library 12, het Fan Museum-Helene Alexander Collection 19 l1,
Victoria & Albert Museum 13.

ISBN 90 246 0169 X
Oorspronkelijke titel: *The Chinese Horoscopes Library – Monkey*
Oorspronkelijke uitgever: Dorling Kindersley, Londen
Copyright © 1994 Dorling Kindersley Limited, Londen
Tekst copyright © 1994 ICOREC

Copyright © 1995 Nederlandse vertaling
Uitgeverij Bosch & Keuning, Baarn
Vertaling: Christien Konijn

Verspreiding voor België:
Uitgeverij Westland nv, Schoten

Gezet door DTQP, Schiedam
Gedrukt en gebonden door Imago, Hongkong

INHOUD

INLEIDING TOT DE CHINESE HOROSCOPEN

Al duizenden jaren hebben de Chinezen hun astrologie en godsdienst gebruikt om een harmonie tot stand te brengen tussen de mens en zijn omgeving.

De juiste herkomst van de twaalf dieren uit de Chinese astrologie, Rat, Buffel,, Tijger, Konijn, Draak, Slang, Paard, Ram, Aap, Haan, Hond en Zwijn, is nog altijd een mysterie. Desondanks zijn deze dieren in de Chinese astrologie van groot belang. Ze betekenen veel meer dan alleen maar een algemene naamgeving aan het jaar of aan mogelijke goede of slechte tijden die ons te wachten staan. De twaalf dieren uit de Chinese astrologie worden beschouwd als een weerspiegeling van het universum.

YIN-EN YANG-SYMBOOL
Wit geeft de vrouwelijke kracht van yin weer, zwart staat voor de mannelijke kracht van yang.

YIN EN YANG

De vele verschillen in onze karakters, stemmingen, gezondheid en geluk geven de grotere veranderingen in het universum weer. De Chinezen geloven

dat alles in het universum in evenwicht wordt gehouden door de stuwende, kosmische krachten van yin en yang. Yin is vrouwelijk, zwak en koel; de kracht van de maan en de regen. Yang is mannelijk, sterk en warm, de kracht van de zon en de aarde. Volgens het oude Chinese geloof vertegenwoordigden de geconcentreerde eigenschappen van yin en yang de vier seizoenen, en de zich verspreidende eigenschappen de talloze schepsels die zich op de aarde bevinden.

De twaalf dieren van de Chinese astrologie zijn allemaal verbonden of met yin, of met yang. De kracht van yin wordt sterker als de winter nadert en neemt af door de warmte van het voorjaar, wanneer yang zich laat gelden.

Zelfs op een gewone dag zijn yin en yang actief, steeds veranderlijk en op zoek naar evenwicht. Ook in onszelf nemen deze krachten toe en af.

Iedereen heeft zijn eigen evenwicht tussen yin en yang. Dit beïnvloedt onze stemmingen, ambities, en gezondheid. Wij reageren ook op weersveranderingen, op de omgeving en op de mensen om ons heen.

DE VIJF ELEMENTEN

Alles wat wij kunnen aanraken, proeven of zien, is verdeeld in vijf basissymbolen of -elementen: hout, vuur, aarde, goud en water. Alles in het universum kan aan een van deze elementen gekoppeld worden. Het element goud bijvoorbeeld is verbonden met de Aap en de Haan. Dit element is ook verbonden met de kleur wit, scherp voedsel, de herfst en gevoelens van verdriet. De activiteit van deze elementen zegt ons iets over onze toekomst.

EEN PERSOONLIJKE ONTDEKKINGSREIS

De Chinese astrologie kan u helpen uw yin en yang in evenwicht te brengen, en kan u ook vertellen welk element bij u hoort, en welke kleuren, smaken, delen van het lichaam of emoties met uw teken verbonden zijn. Aan de hand van het jaar, de maand en het uur waarop u geboren bent, kunt u iets over uw toekomst te weten komen. U kunt erachter komen tot welke personen u zich aangetrokken voelt en welke loopbaan het best bij uw karakter past. U krijgt meer inzicht in uw gemoedswisselingen, uw reacties op bepaalde plekken en op andere mensen. Kortom: langzaam maar zeker ontdekt u wat u tot een individu maakt.

VOORSPELLINGSSTOKJES
Ook een oude en geliefde Chinese manier van toekomst voorspellen is het gebruik van speciale 'voorspellingsstokjes', waarmee men op een heel speciale manier gegevens uit boeken met voorspellingen kan halen.

HET TREKKEN VAN UW HOROSCOOP

De Chinese kalender is gebaseerd op de beweging van de maan; dit in tegenstelling tot de kalender in de westerse wereld, die gebaseerd is op de beweging van de zon.

Zoek, voor u uw Chinese horoscoop trekt, uw geboortejaar op in de tabellen op blz. 44-45. Let vooral goed op als u in de eerste maanden van het jaar geboren bent. Het Chinese jaar begint niet, zoals bij ons, in januari en u zou kunnen horen bij het voorafgaande Chinese jaar. Als u bijvoorbeeld geboren bent in 1961, denkt u misschien dat u in het jaar van de Buffel geboren bent. Als uw verjaardag echter vóór 15 februari valt, behoort u tot het voorafgaande Chinese jaar, het jaar van de Rat.

DE 60-JARIGE CYCLUS

De Chinezen berekenen de tijd in cycli van 60 jaar. De twaalf astrologische dieren verschijnen elk vijf maal gedurende elke 60-jarige cyclus, steeds in een iets andere vorm. Als u bijvoorbeeld geboren bent in 1944, bent u een Aap die een boom inklimt, maar bent u geboren in 1980, dan bent u een Aap in de fruitboom.

MAANDEN, DAGEN EN UREN

De twaalf maanmaanden van de Chinese kalender komen niet precies overeen met de twaalf westerse kalendermaanden. Dat komt omdat de Chinese kalender op de maan gebaseerd is, en de westerse op de zon. De Chinese maanden bevatten meestal 29-30 dagen en elke 3-4 jaar wordt er een extra maand aan toegevoegd, om ongeveer gelijke tred te houden met het westerse jaar.

Een Chinees uur staat gelijk aan twee westerse uren, en de twaalf Chinese uren komen overeen met de twaalf dierentekens.

Jaar, maand, dag en het uur van de geboorte vormen de sleutels tot de Chinese astrologie, en met deze sleutels opent u de deuren tot uw persoonlijke Chinese horoscoop.

	Water
	Aarde		Goud
	Hout		Yin
	Vuur		Yang

CHINEES ASTROLOGISCH WIEL

*In het midden van het wiel ziet u het yin-
en yangsymbool. Daaromheen staan de
Chinese astrologische karakters, die met elk
dier verbonden zijn. De gekleurde rand
onthult uw element, en de buitenste ring
laat zien of u yin of yang bent.*

MYTHEN EN LEGENDEN

Volgens de Chinese legende wilde de Jade Keizer, Yu-ti, de heerser over de hemel, kennismaken met de twaalf belangrijkste dieren. Vervolgens beloonde hij de Aap met de negende plaats.

Apen komen in veel Chinese legenden voor. In Zuid-China gaan er oude verhalen over vrouwen die door apen werden verkracht en vervolgens apejongen ter wereld brachten. Sommige geslachten schrijven hun afkomst toe aan het huwelijk tussen een vrouw en een aap.

DE AAP EN ZIJN VRIENDEN
Op dit 17e-eeuwse muurreliëf uit de grote Pagode in Chengdu, staan apen in diverse gedaantes afgebeeld.

In dit deel van China wordt de aap ook als god vereerd als de 'Grote Wijze Gelijk aan de Hemel'. Maar in de verbeelding van het gewone volk wordt de aap ook in verband gebracht met overspel. Volgens traditie werden afbeeldingen van apen rijdend op paarden cadeau gegeven, met de wens dat de ontvanger snel bevorderd zou worden.

DE LEGENDE VAN DE AAP
In de Chinese novelle *De Reis naar het Westen,* komen ook apen als goden voor.

TWEE APEN VAN JADE

Deze twee prachtige apen van jade houden een perzik vast, het symbool van een lang leven. Ze stammen uit de Chinese Tj'ing-dynastie (1749-1795).

Dit is het bekendste epos in China. Koning Aap, in het Chinees Sun Wu Kung, veroorzaakte veel problemen op aarde, vandaar dat de Jadekeizer, Yu-ti, hem in de hemel uitnodigde en hem daar een 'hemelse' baan aanbood. Dat baantje stelde echter niet veel voor. Woedend ging Koning Aap weer terug naar zijn geliefde apen-leger op de aarde. De Jadekeizer zond hemelse legers achter hem aan, maar Koning Aap versloeg deze allemaal. Opgetogen liet Koning Aap een vaandel maken, waarop geschreven stond 'Grote Wijze Gelijk aan de Hemel'. De onderdanen van Kuan Yin, de Godin van de Barmhartigheid, namen Koning Aap uiteindelijk gevangen, maar Boeddha was de godheid die hem het meest vernederde. Men bracht Koning Aap bij Boeddha. Deze zette hem in zijn hand en zei: 'Ik daag je uit van mijn hand te springen.' Koning Aap lachte en zei: 'Ik kan springen tot aan het einde van het universum.' 'Ga je gang,' zei Boeddha, 'maar laat wel een spoor achter als je daar bent.' Aldus rende Koning Aap miljoenen kilometers tot hij bij de vijf reuzenpilaren arriveerde. Hier schreef hij 'De Grote Wijze Gelijk aan de Hemel was hier' en hij urineerde tegen de middelste pilaar. Toen ging hij terug naar Boeddha's hand en zei: Ik heb gedaan zoals u beval.' 'Maar je hebt mijn hand helemaal niet verlaten, kijk maar,' zei Boeddha. Koning Aap zag zijn woorden geschreven staan op de middelvinger van Boeddha en er hing een sterke urinegeur. Eindelijk wist Koning Aap dat hij zijns gelijke gevonden had.

13

• AAP •
PERSOONLIJKHEID

De Aap is onafhankelijk, slim en menslievend en heeft
daarom een uitstekend aanpassingsvermogen. Hij heeft een
levendige geest en is dol op uitdagingen.

Gevoeligheid is een van uw beste eigenschappen en u leeft mee met andermans problemen. U bent altijd bereid te vechten voor de goede zaak, maar omdat u denkt dat u door uw inspanningen een betere reputatie zult krijgen, bent u ook zeer opportunistisch.

DRIJFVEREN
U bent vrij rusteloos en wordt niet graag aan banden gelegd. U hebt veel bedrijvigheid en afwisseling nodig om aan al uw wensen te kunnen voldoen. Uw scherpe verstand stelt u in staat de situaties snel te beoordelen en daar optimaal van te profiteren. Hoewel u precies weet hoe u de zaken moet regelen en naar uw hand moet zetten, gebruikt u deze talenten op

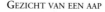

GEZICHT VAN EEN AAP
Deze schelmse figuur van terracotta is afkomstig uit het Verre Oosten en werd gemaakt in de 2e of 3e eeuw.

een wijze manier en zowel uzelf als anderen kunnen van uw schrandere beslissingen profiteren. Wanneer u onder druk wordt gezet of in het nauw wordt gedreven, reageert u snel en slim. Door uw scherpe vernuft weet u zich prima uit moeilijke posities te draaien, zonder uw handen ergens aan vuil te maken.

HET INNERLIJK VAN DE AAP
Uw zelfvertrouwen heeft vaak een zetje nodig en dikwijls verkeert u te midden van een groep mensen, die u vermaakt met uw grote gevoel voor humor en briljante betogen. Soms bent u iets te luidruchtig en te dominant en houdt u geen rekening met de mening van anderen.

14

Veel van dit gedrag vloeit voort uit de vurige wens geaccepteerd en begrepen te worden. Wanneer u zich buitengesloten voelt, bent u diep gekwetst en voelt u zich een mislukkeling. Maar u weet deze onzekere gevoelens goed te verbergen en naar buiten toe lijkt u een luchthartig persoon.

U bent een gulle en gezellige vriend en uw lust en uw leven is voor anderen te zorgen en naar hun problemen te luisteren. U doet altijd uw uiterste best hun moeilijkheden te begrijpen, maar soms kunnen uw gedachten ongewild afdwalen, want u wordt altijd weer geprikkeld door nieuwe ideeën en interesses. Op emotioneel gebied bent u levendig en enthousiast, maar uw relatie moet wel bruisend en boeiend zijn, anders hebt u er snel genoeg van.

U bent een liefdevolle ouder en altijd bereid het enthousiasme van uw kinderen te delen en hun tekortkomingen te dulden.

ZITTENDE AAP

De kleur van jade kan veel schakeringen hebben, van wit tot donkergroen, afhankelijk van het ijzergehalte. Deze bevallige wit-bruine aap van jade werd in de 19de eeuw in China gemaakt.

DE AAP ALS KIND

De jonge Aap heeft een levendige fantasie en past zich zowel op school als thuis prima aan. Maar hij kan heel snel te opgewonden raken en moet misschien aangezet worden wat kalmer te zijn. Het Apekind heeft de neiging nogal kritisch te zijn en zou moeten leren wat meer geduld te hebben.

• AAP •
LIEFDE

De Aap is een charmant schepsel, boordevol intelligentie en enthousiasme. Als hij eenmaal de ware gevonden heeft, zal hij een liefhebbende, toegewijde partner zijn.

In het begin van een relatie bent u dronken van hartstocht en opwinding, maar als de eerste storm geluwd is wordt u kritischer. U kunt niet tegen tekortkomingen en zodra u voelt dat het in uw relatie niet meer goed zit, komt u in de verleiding de benen te nemen. U bent zeer charmant en wil graag aardig zijn, maar uw partner moet wel steeds aandacht schenken aan uw verlangens.

Soms kunt u bestaand geluk zeer abrupt bederven, maar als u iemand ontmoet die u blindelings kunt vertrouwen en die u kan blijven boeien en stimuleren, kunt u een zeer gelukkige relatie hebben. De ideale partners voor u zijn de Rat en de Draak. De wijsheid, hartstocht en het opportunisme van de Rat trekken u aan. Hij moet wel rekening kunnen houden met uw humeur. U en de Draak zullen elkaar bekoorlijk vinden, en de Draak zal verrukt zijn van uw afwisselende bekwaamheden. De Buffel geniet van uw levendigheid en u zult zijn standvastigheid zeer waarderen.

GODIN VAN DE LIEFDE

Kuan Yin is een machtige figuur in de Chinese mythologie. Vroeger was zij een mannelijke boeddhistische godheid, maar nu staat zij bekend als de Godin van Barmhartigheid, en als Sung-tzu, de schenkster van kinderen.

Als het u lukt uw kritiek wat in te binden, zou u goed bij de avontuurlijke Tijger kunnen passen. Uw scherpzinnigheid spreekt het bescheiden Konijn zeer aan, dat u op zijn beurt begrip en tederheid zal schenken. U schept veel genoegen in de gevatheid en intelligentie van een andere Aap, en het eerlijke Zwijn zal uw sluwe streken en snode plannen kunnen aanvoelen. Relaties met de Ram, Hond, Haan, Slang en het Paard zouden veeleisend kunnen zijn. Uw levendigheid wordt gedeeld door de Ram, maar deze zou te veel op u kunnen steunen, en de Hond stoort zich wellicht aan uw zorgeloze aanpak. Hoewel u net zo menslievend bent als de Haan, zult u zelden samen gelukkig

zijn. Uw onvoorspelbaarheid zal de Slang misschien verdriet doen, maar u kunt elkaars intelligentie wel waarderen. Het Paard is overgevoelig en zou u als partner wel eens te hard kunnen vinden.

ORCHIDEE
In China is de orchidee, of Lan Hua, *het symbool van liefde en schoonheid. Zij is ook een symbool van vruchtbaarheid en staat voor veel nakomelingen.*

CHINEES WIEL VAN VERBINDINGEN
Zoek uw dierenteken op en kijk welke dieren dezelfde achtergrondkleur hebben – de Aap heeft een roze achtergrond en is het meest verbonden met de Draak en de Rat. Het karakter in het midden van het wiel betekent 'dubbel geluk'.

• AAP •
LOOPBAAN

De Aap is een noeste werker en heeft behoefte aan afwisseling en uitdagingen. Hij verafschuwt de dagelijkse sleur en voelt zich in een beroep zonder verrassingen zeer opgesloten.

MAKELAAR IN EFFECTEN

Al staat hij nog zo onder druk, de Aap zal altijd de grootste zorg besteden aan zijn financiële en persoonlijke interesses. Daarom zou hij een zeer succesvolle makelaar in effecten kunnen zijn.

Grijs-groene aap

Geld

Fles met heilig water

THEOLOOG

In een loopbaan als theoloog wordt de vaardigheid van de Aap in het leggen van contacten optimaal benut. Bovendien zullen de hoge eisen die een dergelijke studie stelt, aanlokkelijk zijn voor zijn scherpe verstand. Het Chinese grijs-groene beeldje van een aap rechts, stamt uit de 16e of 17e eeuw. Het werd gebruikt als wierookbrander om het contact met de goden te vergemakkelijken.

RAZENDE REPORTER
De Aap heeft een snelle geest, reist graag en is het meest in zijn sas als hij een beroep moet doen op zijn vindingrijkheid. Al deze eigenschappen maken de Aap uiterst geschikt voor een journalistieke loopbaan.

Vliegtuig

ARTISTIEK TEKENAAR
Hoewel de Aap niet bijster bekend staat om zijn artistieke kwaliteiten, is hij toch zeer begaafd. Een beroep in de kunstsector, bijvoorbeeld als kalligraaf, zou dus best iets voor hem kunnen zijn. De letters op deze 19e-eeuwse Chinese waaier zijn geschilderd in goud.

Chinese waaier

Instrument voor een planoloog

Landkaarten

PLANOLOOG
De Aap heeft een buitengewoon scherp oog voor geschikte kansen en is een goede planoloog. Zo nodig kan hij snelle en juiste beslissingen nemen.

GEZONDHEID

*Yin en yang zijn voortdurend in het lichaam in beweging.
Een goede gezondheid is afhankelijk van een constant
evenwicht tussen yin en yang.*

Er is in het menselijk lichaam een natuurlijk maximum- en minimumniveau van yin en yang. De lichaamskracht in het lichaam noemt men tj'i, een yang-kracht. De beweging van tj'i in het menselijk lichaam wordt aangevuld door het stromen van het bloed, een yin-kracht. De minste verstoring van het evenwicht tussen yin en yang in het lichaam kan leiden tot gezondheidsproblemen. Yang-ziekte kan door yin-behandeling worden genezen en vice versa. Iedereen heeft zijn eigen yin- en yang-evenwicht. Het ligt voor de hand dat een heetgebakerd persoon sterke yang-krachten, en een vreedzaam type sterke yin-krachten heeft. Uw karakter is nauw verbonden met uw gezondheid en voor er Chinese medicijnen voorgeschreven worden, moet er veel aandacht geschonken worden aan uw gemoedstoestanden. Er wordt altijd gestreefd naar een evenwicht tussen vreugde, boosheid, verdriet, geluk, zorgen, melancholie en angst. Dit ideale evenwicht staat in China bekend als de Harmonie van de Zeven Gevoelens.

LINGTJIH ZWAM
De zwam, hier afgebeeld op een schaal uit de Tj'ing-dynastie, is de 'onsterfelijke' lingtjih zwam, het symbool van een lang leven.

CHINESE BOKSDOORN
Het binnenste van de schors van dit zeer sterke kruid, wordt in China vaak gebruikt door suikerzieken.

Aangezien u geboren bent in het jaar van de Aap, bent u verbonden met het element goud. Dit element is gekoppeld aan longen, dikke darm, neus, kin en haar. Deze lichaamsdelen zijn van belang voor uw gezondheid. U bent ook verbonden met gevoelens van verdriet en scherp voedsel.

Het binnenste van de schors van de Chinese boksdoorn (*Lycium chinense*) is verbonden met uw Chinese astrologische teken. De zaadjes worden gebruikt voor het herstellen van lever en nieren en bij behandeling van suikerzieken. Het binnenste van de schors wordt vaak toegevoegd aan Chinese yam-soep, die versterkend werkt voor milt, maag, longen en nieren. De soep werkt ook dorstlessend bij suikerzieken.

Chinese medicijnen zijn zeer specifiek, laat u dus nooit verleiden tot het innemen van boksdoorn of welke plant ook, alvorens eerst een deskundige Chinese of westerse arts te raadplegen.

ASTROLOGIE EN ANATOMIE
Uw element goud is vooral verbonden met twee belangrijke organen: de longen en de dikke darm. De longen zijn yin-organen en de dikke darm is een yang-orgaan.

• AAP •
VRIJE TIJD

*De Aap heeft gouden vingers en mag graag dingen maken
of repareren. Hij houdt van afwisseling en uitdagingen,
van boeiende mensen en interessante oorden.*

ROULETTE
*Kansspelen zijn aangename tijdpasseringen
voor de Aap, want hij mag graag een gokje
wagen. Maar hij is ook een ondeugende aap,
en zou best eens vals kunnen spelen om te
winnen.*

Roulette

**Chinees
beeldje van
een aap op
een paardje**

PAARDENRENNEN
*In China gaat het cadeau geven van
een aap, rijdend op een paardje,
gepaard met de wens dat de
ontvanger snel promotie zal maken.
De Aap heeft echter andere banden
met paarden, gewoonlijk in de vorm
van een dag op de races. De Aap
bewondert de vaardigheid van de jockey
en de snelheid van het paard, maar het
voornaamste is dat hij een gokje kan wagen
over de uitslag van de wedstrijd.*

Rijzweep

Narre-schoenen

AMUSEMENT

De Aap is een groot artiest en een geboren clown. Als hij een baan zou hebben aan het hof, zou hij vast de nar zijn. Hij is op zijn best als hij voor het blok gezet wordt, want pas dan kan hij zijn vindingrijkheid botvieren.

Hardloopschoenen

HARDLOPEN

Hoewel de Aap een hekel heeft aan een streng trainingsschema, is hij dol op rennen in de vrije natuur, en wedstrijden en uitdagingen kunnen hem tot enorme prestaties aansporen.

Hand-schoenen voor waterskiërs

Strandbal

WATERSPORTEN

De Aap houdt van alle sporten waar snelheid aan te pas komt, maar is vooral dol op watersporten, zoals waterskiën. Hij zal zich altijd wel vermaken, zelfs met zoiets simpels als een balspel op het strand.

SYMBOLIEK

Elk astrologisch dier is verbonden met een bepaald soort voedsel, een bepaalde richting, kleur, emotie, verbondenheid en symbool. De Aap is ook verbonden met de herfst.

Porseleinen apen

KLEUR
In China is helderwit de kleur van reinheid. Deze kleur is ook verbonden met de Aap. Dit groepje van vier porseleinen apen stamt uit de Tj'ing-dynastie .

Kruidnagels

VOEDSEL
Volgens de Chinese astrologie zijn er vijf smaken: zout, scherp, bitter, zuur en zoet. Scherp voedsel, zoals kruidnagels, is verbonden met de Aap.

Antiek Chinees kompas

Tekenhaak

SYMBOOL
Het symbool van de Aap in de Chinese astrologie is de tekenhaak.

RICHTING
Het Chinese kompas wijst naar het zuiden, terwijl het westerse kompas naar het noorden wijst. De richting van de Aap is het westen.

GEVOELENS
De Aap is verbonden met gevoelens van verdriet.

VERBONDENHEID
Gerechtigheid is verbonden met de Aap.

Vrouwe Justitia en haar weegschaal

Verdrietige baby

AAP DIE EEN BOOM INKLIMT

~ 1944 2004 ~

Deze Aap is in zijn eigen vertrouwde omgeving en heeft het prima naar zijn zin. Hij is verbonden met een uiterst gunstige combinatie, namelijk bomen en succes.

Hoewel de Aap een fortuinlijk teken is, heeft zijn persoonlijkheid ook enige moeilijke kanten. Gelukkig weegt voor de Aap die een boom inklimt het geluk zwaarder dan deze minder gunstige aspecten.

PERSOONLIJKHEID

U bent waarschijnlijk een bijzonder mens. Hiervan zou u uw hele leven profijt van kunnen hebben, maar soms kan het ook frustrerend zijn. Misschien verwijt men u arrogantie, want u denkt dat u, als u de kans krijgt, het veel beter doet dan de mensen in uw omgeving. Zodoende zou men u soms ongeduldig of zelfs lomp kunnen vinden.

U werkt waarschijnlijk niet graag in groepsverband. Probeer geduld te hebben, want uiteindelijk zal men u waarderen om uw capaciteiten en veelzijdigheid en zult u tot volle ontplooiing kunnen komen.

VRIENDSCHAP

Door uw aangeboren dynamische geest bent u een graag geziene vriend. Als u eenmaal het door u beoogde succes hebt behaald, zullen uw vrienden uw gezelschap nog meer waarderen, want dan zult u veel ontspannener zijn.

RELATIES

Tracht in uw gevoelsleven rustig en geduldig te zijn en laat u niet verleiden tot een langdurige verplichting. Misschien duurt het even voor u de ware ontmoet, maar als u die eenmaal gevonden hebt, kunt u het samen heel gezellig hebben.

OUDERSCHAP

Misschien krijgt u pas op latere leeftijd kinderen, en dat is wel zo goed. Als u namelijk eenmaal uw doel bereikt hebt, zult u beter in staat zijn uw gezinsleden die steun en aandacht te geven die zij nodig hebben en verdienen.

Aap die een boom inklimt

VOORUITZICHTEN

Naarmate u ouder wordt, zal men u meer gaan waarderen. Dan zult u vele successen boeken en een aangenaam leven leiden. Uw ontwikkeling door het leven zal steeds soepeler verlopen. Houd echter altijd dat typische Apetrekje in de gaten, namelijk leugentjes om bestwil vertellen. Dit achterbakse karaktertrekje zou al uw geluk teniet kunnen doen, probeer dit dus altijd goed onder controle te houden.

AAP DIE DE BERG BEKLIMT

~ 1956 2016 ~

Deze Aap houdt van de uitdaging een berg te beklimmen.
Aangezien hij echter uit zijn natuurlijke omgeving is, zou
dit avontuur ook veel spanningen kunnen veroorzaken.

U bent verbonden met de huiselijke haard. Symbolisch gezien betekent dit dat u tot verwennen en troosten in staat bent, maar ook tot branden en vernietigen. Probeer dan ook in alle fasen van uw leven zorgvuldigheid en zelfbeheersing te betrachten.

U hebt veel in uw mars en uw toekomst ziet er rooskleurig uit. U zult echter ook het hoofd moeten bieden aan gevaren. Probeer het rechte pad te houden, dan zult u vast successen boeken.

PERSOONLIJKHEID
Uw grootste probleem is uw neiging overspannen te raken. De meeste Apen denken dat ze elke uitdaging op hun sloffen aankunnen – zelfs het beklimmen van een berg. Probeer echter goed voor uzelf te zorgen. Ondanks het feit dat u van uitdagingen geniet, bent u niet altijd bij machte deze met gemak en succesvol aan te gaan. Probeer de grenzen die er zijn aan uw krachten,

capaciteiten en verstand te accepteren en leer nieuwe mogelijkheden wat behoedzamer tegemoet te treden. Zolang u het hoofd koel houdt en alleen die kansen en uitdagingen oppakt die u echt aankunt, zult u veel succes kunnen hebben.

RELATIES
Laat op het emotionele vlak het roekeloze en eigenzinnige karaktertrekje van de Aap uw doen en laten niet bepalen. Het is voor u van groot belang precies te weten welke risico's u wilt nemen in uw contacten met uw partners, zowel in uw privé-leven als op uw werk. Onthoud goed dat, als u verleid wordt tot affaires en avontuurtjes buiten deze relaties, u daar uiteindelijk zelf het meeste onder te lijden zult hebben.

Aap die de berg beklimt

VOORUITZICHTEN

Elk financieel voordeeltje moet met zorg worden behandeld. Laat u niet verleiden dit extraatje gelijk over de balk te gooien, want misschien doet zo'n meevaller zich nooit meer voor. Bekijk liever eerst eens de vele mogelijkheden van investeren en verheug u op later, wanneer u ervan kunt gaan profiteren. Anderen zullen deze verstandige handelwijze respecteren, en in uw latere leven zult u misschien zelfs roem en rijkdom kunnen verwerven. In u schuilt altijd een combinatie van capaciteiten en gevaren – dezelfde krachten en vaardigheden waarvan u zoveel profijt hebt, kunnen ook vernietigend werken. Zolang u dit goed in de gaten houdt, zult u leren hoeveel plezier u kunt hebben van uw warme en aangename persoonlijkheid. Als u daarentegen onvoorzichtig bent, kunt u uzelf of anderen veel verdriet doen.

EENZAME AAP

~ 1908 1968 ~

*Ondanks zijn zielige naam, hoeft de Eenzame Aap
helemaal niet treurig te zijn. Helaas zal hij wel gebukt
gaan onder moeilijkheden in de familiekring.*

U bent verbonden met hakken, en zult daarom maar al te gemakkelijk mensen de grond in 'hakken'.

PERSOONLIJKHEID

Al uw problemen staan waarschijnlijk in verband met deze persoonlijke zwakheid. U zegt altijd precies wat u denkt. U zou misschien iets inschikkelijker en wat minder met uzelf bezig kunnen zijn. Van nature bent u snel van geest en zeer intelligent. Deze overdaad moet echter in de hand worden gehouden, want in contacten met familie en vrienden hebt u er weinig profijt van.

U hebt nogal last van ups en downs en hoewel deze wisselende stemmingen u misschien zorgen baren, zullen anderen deze zeker als nog schokkender en verwarrender ervaren. U wordt altijd makkelijk beïnvloed door mensen en omstandigheden. Probeer dit onder controle te houden.

FAMILIE

Helaas zult u in familiekring veel moeilijkheden ondervinden. Uw verhouding met uw ouders kan er waarschijnlijk net mee door, maar tussen u en uw kinderen zouden levensgrote problemen kunnen rijzen. De kans is groot dat uw broers en/of zusters u een echte apekop vinden, met wie moeilijk valt om te gaan.

VOORUITZICHTEN

U bent een harde werker. Hiervoor wordt u op diverse manieren beloond. Op financieel gebied zijn deze beloningen redelijk, maar niet overdreven. Gelukkig kunt u van nature goed met geld omgaan, zodat u financieel gezien geen zorgen hoeft te hebben.

De combinatie van uw aangeboren intelligentie, natuurlijke ijver en het vermogen uitdagingen aan te kunnen gaan, zou de aandacht kunnen trekken

Eenzame Aap

van mensen in hoge posities. Zij zullen uw vele kwaliteiten in de gaten hebben en proberen u vooruit te helpen. U moet echter wel uw scherpe tong in bedwang houden, want vooral hoogstaande personen zouden deze hoogst irritant en provocerend kunnen vinden.

Vergeet nooit dat u verbonden bent met hakken, hetgeen inhoudt dat elke nieuwe fase in uw leven op elk moment, ja zelfs al in het begin, bruut afgebroken zou kunnen worden door een ondoordachte daad.

Zolang u deze karaktertrek niet uit het oog verliest en u uw stemmingen weet te beheersen, zullen de contacten met familie en collega's stukken beter worden.

AAP IN DE FRUITBOOM

~ 1920 1980 ~

Deze Aap wordt omringd door de heerlijkste vruchten, en niets kan hem stoppen zijn hart op te halen. Helaas is het leven niet altijd zo volmaakt als het lijkt.

U bent verbonden met twee opgeheven handen die een schaal vasthouden. Soms wordt dit beschouwd als gelijke alternatieven, of als de twee verschillende zijden van een en dezelfde munt. Dit zou de indruk kunnen wekken dat de motieven achter uw daden niet altijd hoeven te stroken met de manier waarop anderen deze ervaren.

PERSOONLIJKHEID

Ondanks uw onberispelijke en edelmoedige gedrag zal men u niet gauw lof toezwaaien of uw daden waarderen. Dit kan zonder meer frustrerend zijn, maar raak hierdoor niet verbitterd. Vergeet niet dat u door het leven fladdert, en uitstekende kansen hebt op succes en geluk. Anderen zullen dit waarschijnlijk niet erg waarderen, maar geef nooit toe aan gevoelens van minachting of cynisme, want dat zou schadelijk voor u kunnen zijn. U bent vast heel aantrekkelijk en men ervaart u als kwiek en blijmoedig. Men zou echter ook wel eens jaloers op u kunnen zijn. In dit geval kunt u het beste trouw aan uzelf blijven.

VROUWELIJKE KENMERKEN

De vrouwelijke Aap in de fruitboom heeft bijzonder veel last van jaloezie. Deze kan komen van haar vrienden, of zelfs van haar medegezinsleden, die misschien vinden dat alleen aan haar al het geluk en de bekoorlijkheid ten deel is gevallen.

VRIENDSCHAP

Wonderlijk genoeg zouden geluk en succes gevoelens van eenzaamheid en verlatenheid bij u kunnen oproepen. Schenk dus altijd voldoende aandacht aan vriendschappen en ga er nooit van uit dat deze zonder meer in stand zullen blijven.

Aap in de fruitboom

VOORUITZICHTEN

Hoewel uw meerderen u zelden zullen prijzen, zullen ze uiteindelijk uw nauwkeurigheid gaan waarderen en u allerlei kansen bieden. Zolang u maar elke uitdaging aangaat die u geboden wordt, zal uw loopbaan op rolletjes lopen. Aangezien de Aap in de fruitboom een geluksvogel is, moet u proberen elke kans te grijpen die u krijgt.

SIERLIJKE AAP

~ 1932 1992 ~

Deze Aap zit ingewikkeld in elkaar, en is geneigd een hoge
pet van zichzelf op te hebben. Soms wordt de Sierlijke Aap
beschuldigd van arrogantie.

U hebt een uitgesproken talent uw opbrengsten te doen stijgen. Dit betekent grote voorspoed, want u ziet winst te halen uit alles wat u aanpakt en voelt precies aan wanneer u het beste kunt oogsten wat u hebt gezaaid.

PERSOONLIJKHEID

Soms lijkt uw karakter enigszins tegenstrijdig. U bent zeer intelligent, hetgeen tot een overdreven zelfverzekerd, opschepperig gedrag kan leiden, maar u kunt ook zeer beminnelijk zijn.
Het natuurlijke gevolg van deze tegenstrijdigheid is dat u onderhevig bent aan stemmingen. U bent altijd zeer uitbundig, maar als iemand door uw impulsieve gedrag overstuur raakt, voelt u zich ellendig. Deze wisselende stemmingen maken u soms depressief, dus probeer ze onder controle te houden. De beste oplossing is misschien uw hersens erbij te houden, en de problemen door uw aangeboren vriendelijkheid iets

af te zwakken. Probeer uw ingewikkelde persoonlijkheid te accepteren. Zelf-aanvaarding kan een prima hulpmiddel zijn en u komt er ooit nog wel eens achter hoe u deze tegenstrijdigheid het beste kunt hanteren.
In financiële zaken bent u behoedzaam, maar u kunt dit ook overdrijven, en zelfs van gierigheid worden beschuldigd. Let hierop, want dat kan uiteindelijk tot problemen leiden. Anderen zouden zich niet meer bij u op hun gemak kunnen voelen, of twijfelen aan uw goede bedoelingen.
Vergeet niet dat zuinigheid weliswaar niet verkeerd is, maar ga niet zo ver dat deze eigenschap leidt tot overdreven ongenaakbaarheid en krenterigheid.

Sierlijke Aap

LOOPBAAN

Uw kwieke persoonlijkheid kan leiden tot roem, maar denk altijd aan de ongewenste aandacht die het genadeloze licht van de schijnwerpers op u kan vestigen.

RELATIES

Als u uw partner met zorg uitkiest, kunt u een uitstekende, hechte relatie hebben. Als u eenmaal de juiste keuze hebt gemaakt, zal uw partner waarschijnlijk zeer trouw en ondersteunend zijn. Uw

kinderen zullen ongetwijfeld profiteren van uw goede positie en u zult altijd trots op hen zijn.

VOORUITZICHTEN

U hebt veel in uw mars. Als u leert zich volwassen te gedragen, maar ook uitdagingen en opwinding niet uit de weg gaat, kunt u het ver schoppen. Omdat u verbonden bent met roem en succes, kunt u daar meer van genieten dan de meeste mensen.

Uw Chinese
GEBOORTEMAAND

Zoek in de tabel uw geboortejaar op en kijk wat uw Chinese geboortemaand is. Als u bijvoorbeeld op 30 augustus 1956 geboren bent, bent u geboren in de zevende Chinese maand.

1 U houdt van uitdagingen. Probeer naar anderen te luisteren en stort u niet in romantische avontuurtjes.

2 U houdt u aan uw woord, maar kunt slecht situaties beoordelen. Wees voorzichtig op het emotionele vlak.

3 U geniet van het leven. Wees op uw werk niet te slordig, want dit zou u uw baan kunnen kosten.

4 U bent een harde werker en wordt door anderen zeer gewaardeerd. U hebt een sterk rechtvaardigheidsgevoel.

5 U verkeert liever in dromenland dan in de harde wereld. Probeer realistisch te zijn en gebruik uw gezonde verstand.

6 U bent talentvol en zou successen kunnen boeken. U bent echter ook onderhevig aan stemmingen.

7 U bent eerlijk, een harde werker en elegant. Gewoonlijk dwarrelt u als een vlindertje door het leven.

8 U bent creatief, maar kunt ook ernstig en moraliserend zijn. Tracht wat minder snel te oordelen.

9 U bent nerveus en gauw bang. Probeer uw neiging in een hoekje te willen kruipen te onderdrukken.

10 U houdt alles graag in de hand. Uw enorme energie maakt u zeer geliefd.

11 U bent openhartig en uniek. Naarmate u ouder wordt zal deze onalledaagsheid meer worden gewaardeerd.

12 U bent nauwkeurig en attent, maar uw persoonlijkheid heeft ook een mysterieus kantje.

---

* Sommige Chinese jaren bevatten dubbele maanden:

1944 : maand 4	1968 : maand 7
23 apr – 21 mei	25 juli – 23 aug
22 mei – 20 juni	24 aug – 21 sept

2004 : maand 2
20 febr – 20 mrt
21 mrt – 18 apr

1908	
2 febr – 2 mrt	1
3 mrt – 31 mrt	2
1 apr – 29 apr	3
30 apr – 29 mei	4
30 mei – 28 juni	5
29 juni – 27 juli	6
28 juli – 26 aug	7
27 aug – 24 sept	8
25 sept – 24 okt	9
25 okt – 23 nov	10
24 nov – 22 dec	11
23 dec – 21 jan 1909	12

1920	
20 febr – 19 mrt	1
20 mrt – 18 apr	2
19 apr – 17 mei	3
18 mei – 15 juni	4
16 juni – 15 juli	5
16 juli – 13 aug	6
14 aug – 11 sept	7
12 sept – 11 okt	8
12 okt – 9 nov	9
10 nov – 9 dec	10
10 dec – 8 jan 1921	11
9 jan – 7 febr	12

1932	
6 febr – 6 mrt	1
7 mrt – 5 apr	2
6 april – 5 mei	3
6 mei – 3 juni	4
4 juni – 3 juli	5
4 juli – 1 aug	6
2 aug – 31 aug	7
1 sept – 29 sept	8
30 sept – 28 okt	9
29 okt – 27 nov	10
28 nov – 26 dec	11
27 dec – 25 jan 1933	12

1944	
25 jan – 23 febr	1
24 febr – 23 mrt	2
24 mrt – 22 apr	3
*zie tabel dubbele maanden	4
21 juni – 19 juli	5
20 juli – 18 aug	6
19 aug – 16 sept	7
17 sept – 16 okt	8
17 okt – 15 nov	9
16 nov – 14 dec	10
15 dec – 13 jan 1945	11
14 jan – 12 febr	12

1956	
12 febr – 11 mrt	1
12 mrt – 10 apr	2
11 apr – 9 mei	3
10 mei – 8 juni	4
9 juni – 7 juli	5
8 juli – 5 aug	6
6 aug – 4 sept	7
5 sept – 3 okt	8
4 okt – 2 nov	9
3 nov – 1 dec	10
2 dec – 31 dec	11
1 jan – 30 jan 1957	12

1968	
30 jan – 27 febr	1
28 febr – 28 mrt	2
29 mrt – 26 apr	3
27 apr – 26 mei	4
27 mei – 25 juni	5
26 juni – 24 juli	6
*zie tabel dubbele maanden	7
22 sept – 21 okt	8
22 okt – 19 nov	9
20 nov – 19 dec	10
20 dec – 17 jan 1969	11
18 jan – 16 febr	12

1980	
16 febr – 16 mrt	1
17 mrt – 14 apr	2
15 apr – 13 mei	3
14 mei – 12 juni	4
13 juni – 11 juli	5
12 juli – 10 aug	6
11 aug – 8 sept	7
9 sept – 8 okt	8
9 okt – 7 nov	9
8 nov – 6 dec	10
7 dec – 5 jan 1981	11
6 jan – 4 febr	12

1992	
4 febr – 3 mrt	1
4 mrt – 2 apr	2
3 apr – 2 mei	3
3 mei – 31 mei	4
1 juni – 29 juni	5
30 juni – 29 juli	6
30 juli – 27 aug	7
28 aug – 25 sept	8
26 sept – 25 okt	9
26 okt – 23 nov	10
24 nov – 23 dec	11
24 dec – 22 jan 1993	12

2004	
22 jan – 19 febr	1
* zie tabel dubbele maanden	2
19 apr – 18 mei	3
19 mei – 17 juni	4
18 juni – 16 juli	5
17 juli – 15 aug	6
16 aug – 13 sept	7
14 sept – 13 okt	8
14 okt – 11 nov	9
12 nov – 11 dec	10
12 dec – 9 jan 2005	11
10 jan – 8 febr	12

Uw Chinese
GEBOORTEDAG

Zoek op de vorige bladzijde uw Chinese geboortemaand op,
reken daarna aan de hand van onderstaande tabel uw
Chinese geboortedag uit.

Als u bent geboren op 5 mei 1908, valt uw verjaardag in de maand die begint op 30 april. Zoek op onderstaande tabel 30 op. Neem 30 als de eerste dag en tel verder tot u bij uw geboortedatum bent. Denk eraan, dat niet alle maanden 31 dagen bevatten. U bent geboren op de 6e dag van de Chinese maand. Als u in een dubbele Chinese maand geboren bent, tel dan gewoon de dagen vanaf de eerste datum van de maand waarin u geboren bent.

1	2	3	4	5	6	7
8	9	10	11	12	13	14
15	16	17	18	19	20	21
22	23	24	25	26	27	28
29	30	31				

Dag 1, 10, 19 of 28
U bent betrouwbaar, stelt hoge eisen, maar bent geneigd uw plannen overhaast uit te voeren. Tracht voorzichtig te zijn en verg niet te veel van uzelf. Er bestaat een kans dat u onverwacht geld ontvangt, maar houd uw uitgaven in de gaten. U bent geschikt voor een baan in de openbare sector of in de kunst.

Dag 2, 11, 20 of 29
U bent eerlijk en populair. U hebt rust nodig, maar houdt ook van geanimeerd gezelschap. Soms hebt u last van woedeuitbarstingen. U bent geneigd van het leven te genieten en uw mogelijkheden optimaal te benutten. Een literaire of kunstzinnige loopbaan is voor u uitermate geschikt.

Dag 3, 12, 21 of 30
U bent vlug van begrip, maar komt soms wat moeilijk over, met als gevolg dat u moeilijk vrienden maakt. U bent zeer gedisciplineerd en hebt de waarheid hoog in het vaandel staan. Een loopbaan

waarin strijd geleverd moet worden is voor u zeer geschikt.

Dag 4, 13, 22 of 31

U bent zeer hartelijk, maar kunt ook gereserveerd zijn, zodat u soms ongenaakbaar lijkt. Als u probeert iets vriendelijker en socialer te zijn, zal men u een stuk aardiger vinden. U bent rustig en geduldig en een baan als wetenschapper of onderzoeker zal goed bij u passen.

Dag 5, 14 of 23

Door uw trotse, koppige aard kunt u soms moeilijk ideeën of meningen van anderen accepteren en uw eigenzinnigheid kan leiden tot meningsverschillen of problemen. U hebt waarschijnlijk geluk met geld en zult dit vaak gebruiken voor het opzetten van nieuwe projecten. Door uw aangeboren intelligentie bent u opgewassen tegen veeleisende taken.

Dag 6, 15 of 24

U bent open, evenwichtig en opgewekt van aard en geniet van een druk sociaal leven. U bent hartelijk en emotioneel en geneigd tot dagdromen. Dit kan leiden tot verwarring, en uw enthousiasme om anderen te helpen kan door uw besluiteloosheid worden afgeremd. Hoewel u nooit echt rijk zult worden, hebt u altijd geld genoeg.

Dag 7, 16 of 25

U houdt van een zekere opwinding in uw leven, maar u moet leren met beide benen op de grond te blijven staan. U bent en geboren toneelspeler, maar pas op dat u niet te veel vervreemdt van uw vrienden of collega's. In uw werk is de mogelijkheid tot reizen belangrijker dan een goed salaris of een hoge levensstandaard.

Dag 8, 17 of 26

U kunt goed een oordeel vellen, maar moet niet te snel handelen. Uw sociale vaardigheden laten soms te wensen over en dat kan anderen wel eens afschrikken. Tracht dus iets tactvoller te zijn. U zult armoede meemaken, maar ook rijkdom. Uw rustige en vastberaden karakter wordt gecombineerd met een levendige geest, waardoor u uitermate geschikt bent om iets voor uzelf te beginnen.

Dag 9, 18 of 27

U bent gelukkig, optimistisch en hartelijk. U bent altijd in de weer en houdt zich niet bezig met alledaagse onbeduidendheden. Soms maakt u onnodig ruzie met uw vrienden en het is van belang dat u leert zich te beheersen. U bent uiterst geschikt voor een baan als directeur of eigenaar.

UW CHINESE GEBOORTEUUR

In de Chinese tijd is een uur gelijk aan twee westerse uren. Elk dubbel Chinees uur is verbonden met een van de twaalf astrologische dieren.

 23.00 – 01.00 UUR
HET UUR VAN DE RAT
U bent onafhankelijk en heftig van aard. Tracht tot tien te tellen voor u uw mond opendoet. Uw zuinigheid zal nuttig zijn, zowel zakelijk als privé. U bent altijd bereid uw naasten te helpen en zij zullen u uw steun met gelijke munt terugbetalen.

 01.00 – 03.00 UUR
HET UUR VAN DE BUFFEL
Tot uw twintigste was uw leven wellicht problematisch, maar daarna lacht het geluk u waarschijnlijk toe. In uw loopbaan moet u bedacht zijn op het nemen van risico's en u zult het ouderlijk huis al vroeg moeten verlaten om te scoren in het leven. U zult van een welvarende oude dag genieten.

03.00 – 05.00 UUR
HET UUR VAN DE TIJGER
U bent levendig en creatief, hetgeen tijdens uw jeugd tot familieruzies kan leiden. Tussen uw twintigste en

veertigste kunt u veel problemen hebben. Gelukkig zal alles na uw veertigste beter gaan.

05.00 – 07.00 UUR
HET UUR VAN HET KONIJN
Uw ouders zijn misschien wel behulpzaam, maar uw broers of zusters kunnen uw rivalen zijn. Misschien moet u het huis wel uit om uw werk optimaal te kunnen doen. Het zou even kunnen duren voor uw relatie standvastig is, maar na uw middelbare leeftijd zult u met iedereen beter kunnen opschieten.

07.00 UUR – 09.00 UUR
HET UUR VAN DE DRAAK
U bent vlug van begrip, vastberaden en aantrekkelijk. U zult een druk leven hebben, maar soms ook eenzaam zijn. U bereikt een hoge levensstandaard. Probeer uw overdreven zelfvertrouwen enigszins te beteugelen, want dat zou moeilijkheden in een relatie kunnen geven.

09.00 – 11.00 UUR
HET UUR VAN DE SLANG

U hebt een goede neus voor zaken doen en zult met gemak een loopbaan opbouwen waarmee u uw gezin kunt onderhouden. U hebt een groot hart en zult met veel plezier uw vrienden helpen als ze in moeilijkheden zijn. Helaas verlopen uw familiecontacten niet altijd even gesmeerd.

11.00 – 13.00 UUR
HET UUR VAN HET PAARD

U bent actief, slim en eigenzinnig. Probeer naar adviezen van anderen te luisteren. U houdt veel van reizen en van een afwisselend leven. Tracht uw uitspattingen onder controle te houden.

13.00 – 15.00 UUR
HET UUR VAN DE RAM

Omdat u zeer actief bent, hebt u moeite uw betrekkingen met familie en vrienden in evenwicht te houden. U bent slim, maar moet anderen uw denkbeelden niet opdringen. Op middelbare leeftijd zou u met enige tegenslag te kampen kunnen krijgen.

15.00 – 17.00 UUR
HET UUR VAN DE AAP

U hebt geen moeite met het verdienen en uitgeven van geld. U hebt een lief karakter, maar bent frustrerend voor anderen. Soms geven uw ouders u niet genoeg morele steun. Uw relatie zit wel goed, maar tob niet te lang over emotionele problemen, want dat kan een negatieve invloed hebben op uw werk.

17.00 – 19.00 UUR
HET UUR VAN DE HAAN

Als puber komt u waarschijnlijk vaak in opstand tegen uw medegezinsleden. Dit zou zelfs kunnen leiden tot een breuk in het gezin, die uiteindelijk wel weer gelijmd wordt. U bent betrouwbaar, vriendelijk en hartelijk en u zult geen vlieg kwaad doen.

19.00 – 21.00 UUR
HET UUR VAN DE HOND

U hebt lef en veel capaciteiten, en bent een harde werker, zodat u uitermate geschikt bent een eigen zaak te leiden. Uw loopbaan ziet er rooskleurig uit. Tracht uw ongeduld en ijdelheid in toom te houden. De kwaliteit van uw leven is u veel meer waard dan een hoge bankrekening.

21.00 – 23.00 UUR
HET UUR VAN HET ZWIJN

U bent zeer handig met de vingers en stelt hoge eisen aan uzelf. Hoewel u een hartelijk mens bent, houdt u niet van te veel vrienden om u heen. Uw intimi vertrouwt u blindelings. Onbekenden brengen u gemakkelijk van uw stuk, maar u kunt snel vergeten en vergeven.

UW LOT IN
ANDERE DIERENJAREN

Wat de Aap te wachten staat gedurende de twaalf dierenjaren wisselt steeds. Richt u vooral op de positieve aspecten van een jaar en ga voorzichtig om met de negatieve zaken die op uw pad kunnen komen.

HET JAAR VAN DE RAT

Hoewel u in het jaar van de Rat succes zult hebben, kunt u daar niet optimaal van genieten. Dit komt in hoofdzaak doordat u achtervolgd wordt door uw verleden. Pas als u uw innerlijke conflicten hebt opgelost, zal het beter met u gaan.

HET JAAR VAN DE BUFFEL

Dit is een zeer gunstig jaar, zowel in familiekring als op uw werk. U zult wel met wat problemen te kampen krijgen, maar die zijn klein en zullen op geen enkele manier het succes en geluk in het jaar van de Buffel in de weg staan.

HET JAAR VAN DE TIJGER

In huiselijke kring zullen er wat problemen zijn, waardoor u gedwongen wordt op reis te gaan. Gedurende uw reizen zult u uw financiële problemen het hoofd kunnen bieden, met als gevolg dat het aan het thuisfront ook weer wat soepeler zal gaan.

HET JAAR VAN HET KONIJN

In het jaar van het Konijn loopt alles wat u aanpakt gesmeerd. Anderen zullen zich afvragen hoe u zo plotseling aan die gouden handen komt, maar u krijgt gewoon wat u verdient.

HET JAAR VAN DE DRAAK

Uw geluk is nogal wisselend en u zult zich zeer onzeker voelen. Maar het jaar van de Draak zal u ook, uit een onverwachte hoek, succes brengen. U bent dit jaar gevoelig voor ongelukken, wees dus voorzichtig en denk goed na voor u iets onderneemt.

HET JAAR VAN DE SLANG

Hoewel u in het jaar van de Slang bij uw vrienden in een goed blaadje zult staan, zult u meer moeilijkheden hebben dan normaal. De grondoorzaak voor deze problemen is waarschijnlijk dat u bij andere mensen wrevel opwekt.

HET JAAR VAN HET PAARD

Gedurende dit moeilijke jaar zal een onophoudelijke stroom van beproevingen en rampspoeden u achtervolgen. Blijf kalm, en bedenk dat zolang u waakzaam en voorzichtig bent, sommige van deze problemen vermeden kunnen worden.

HET JAAR VAN DE RAM

Helaas is dit niet een van de betere jaren voor de Aap. U sukkelt vooral met uw gezondheid. Ziektes zullen u afmatten, en u zult zich gefrustreerd en eenzaam voelen. Probeer dus extra goed voor uzelf te zorgen.

HET JAAR VAN DE AAP

Dit is uw eigen jaar, en u hebt er wellicht hoge verwachtingen van. Hierin wordt u niet teleurgesteld en u zult de depressies van het afgelopen jaar geheel te boven komen. Vriendschappen zullen heel waardevol zijn, doe dus uw best deze weer op te bouwen.

HET JAAR VAN DE HAAN

In alle opzichten moet u erg oppassen, want dit jaar zal voor u waarschijnlijk uitzonderlijk moeilijk en veeleisend zijn. Probeer uw beste beentje voor te zetten en kies vrienden en kennissen met zorg uit.

HET JAAR VAN DE HOND

Uw gedrag zou gedurende het jaar van de Hond veel verdriet kunnen veroorzaken. Misschien wordt u zelf door dit verdriet getroffen, maar het kan ook andere mensen treffen. In ieder geval zal dit jaar waarschijnlijk moeilijk, afmattend en verwarrend zijn.

HET JAAR VAN HET ZWIJN

In dit jaar moet u grote terughoudendheid betrachten in al uw financiële zaken. Misschien wordt u in de verleiding gebracht uitzonderlijk veel te reizen. Tracht hieraan weerstand te bieden, want het zal u duur komen te staan, zowel op emotioneel als op financieel gebied.

Uw Chinese
GEBOORTEJAAR

Uw astrologisch dier stemt overeen met uw Chinese geboortejaar. Het is de belangrijkste sleutel die de deur opent tot uw persoonlijke horoscoop.

Zoek uw westerse geboortejaar op in de linkerkolom van de tabel. In de rechterkolom vindt u op dezelfde regel uw Chinese astrologische dier. Als u in het begin van het jaar geboren bent, kijk dan goed naar de middelste kolom. Als u bijvoorbeeld geboren bent in 1969, denkt u misschien dat u hoort bij het jaar van de Haan. Als uw verjaardag echter valt vóór 17 februari behoort u tot het jaar van de Aap.

1900	31 jan – 18 febr 1901	Rat	1917	23 jan – 10 febr 1918	Slang
1901	19 febr – 7 febr 1902	Buffel	1918	11 febr – 31 jan 1919	Paard
1902	8 febr – 28 jan 1903	Tijger	1919	1 febr – 19 febr 1920	Ram
1903	29 jan – 15 febr 1904	Konijn	1920	20 febr – 7 febr 1921	Aap
1904	16 febr – 3 febr 1905	Draak	1921	8 febr – 27 jan 1922	Haan
1905	4 febr – 24 jan 1906	Slang	1922	28 jan – 15 febr 1923	Hond
1906	25 jan – 12 febr 1907	Paard	1923	16 febr – 4 febr 1924	Zwijn
1907	13 febr – 1 febr 1908	Ram	1924	5 febr – 23 jan 1925	Rat
1908	2 febr – 21 jan 1909	Aap	1925	24 jan – 12 febr 1926	Buffel
1909	22 jan – 9 febr 1910	Haan	1926	13 febr – 1 febr 1927	Tijger
1910	10 febr – 29 jan 1911	Hond	1927	2 febr – 22 jan 1928	Konijn
1911	30 jan – 17 febr 1912	Zwijn	1928	23 febr – 9 febr 1929	Draak
1912	18 febr – 5 febr 1913	Rat	1929	10 febr – 29 jan 1930	Slang
1913	6 febr – 25 jan 1914	Buffel	1930	30 jan – 16 febr 1931	Paard
1914	26 jan – 13 febr 1915	Tijger	1931	17 febr – 5 febr 1932	Ram
1915	14 febr – 2 febr 1916	Konijn	1932	6 febr – 25 jan 1933	Aap
1916	3 febr – 22 jan 1917	Draak	1933	26 jan – 13 febr 1934	Haan

1934	14 febr – 3 febr 1935	Hond	1971	27 jan – 14 febr 1972	Zwijn
1935	4 febr – 23 jan 1936	Zwijn	1972	15 febr – 2 febr 1973	Rat
1936	24 jan – 10 febr 1937	Rat	1973	3 febr – 22 jan 1974	Buffel
1937	11 febr – 30 jan 1938	Buffel	1974	23 jan – 10 febr 1975	Tijger
1938	31 jan – 18 febr 1939	Tijger	1975	11 febr – 30 jan 1976	Konijn
1939	19 febr – 7 febr 1940	Konijn	1976	31 jan – 17 febr 1977	Draak
1940	8 febr – 26 jan 1941	Draak	1977	18 febr – 6 febr 1978	Slang
1941	27 jan – 14 febr 1942	Slang	1978	7 febr – 27 jan 1979	Paard
1942	15 febr – 4 febr 1943	Paard	1979	28 jan – 15 febr 1980	Ram
1943	5 febr – 24 jan 1944	Ram	1980	16 febr – 4 febr 1981	Aap
1944	25 jan – 12 febr 1945	Aap	1981	5 febr – 24 jan 1982	Haan
1945	13 febr – 1 febr 1946	Haan	1982	25 jan – 12 febr 1983	Hond
1946	2 febr – 21 jan 1947	Hond	1983	13 febr – 1 febr 1984	Zwijn
1947	22 jan – 9 febr 1948	Zwijn	1984	2 febr – 19 febr 1985	Rat
1948	10 febr – 28 jan 1949	Rat	1985	20 febr – 8 febr 1986	Buffel
1949	29 jan – 16 febr 1950	Buffel	1986	9 febr – 28 jan 1987	Tijger
1950	17 febr – 5 febr 1951	Tijger	1987	29 jan – 16 febr 1988	Konijn
1951	6 febr – 26 jan 1952	Konijn	1988	17 febr – 5 febr 1989	Draak
1952	27 jan – 13 febr 1953	Draak	1989	6 febr – 26 jan 1990	Slang
1953	14 febr – 2 febr 1954	Slang	1990	27 jan – 14 febr 1991	Paard
1954	3 febr – 23 jan 1955	Paard	1991	15 febr – 3 febr 1992	Ram
1955	24 jan – 11 febr 1956	Ram	1992	4 febr – 22 jan 1993	Aap
1956	12 febr – 30 jan 1957	Aap	1993	23 jan – 9 febr 1994	Haan
1957	31 jan – 17 febr 1958	Haan	1994	10 febr – 30 jan 1995	Hond
1958	18 febr – 7 febr 1959	Hond	1995	31 jan – 18 febr 1996	Zwijn
1959	8 febr – 27 jan 1960	Zwijn	1996	19 febr – 6 febr 1997	Rat
1960	28 jan – 14 febr 1961	Rat	1997	7 febr – 27 jan 1998	Buffel
1961	15 febr – 4 febr 1962	Buffel	1998	28 jan – 15 febr 1999	Tijger
1962	5 febr – 24 jan 1963	Tijger	1999	16 febr – 4 febr 2000	Konijn
1963	25 jan – 12 febr 1964	Konijn	2000	5 febr – 23 jan 2001	Draak
1964	13 febr – 1 febr 1965	Draak	2001	24 jan – 11 febr 2002	Slang
1965	2 febr – 20 jan 1966	Slang	2002	12 febr – 31 jan 2003	Paard
1966	21 jan – 8 febr 1967	Paard	2003	1 febr – 21 jan 2004	Ram
1967	9 febr – 29 jan 1968	Ram	2004	22 jan – 8 febr 2005	Aap
1968	30 jan – 16 febr 1969	Aap	2005	9 febr – 28 jan 2006	Haan
1969	17 febr – 5 febr 1970	Haan	2006	29 jan – 17 febr 2007	Hond
1970	6 febr – 26 jan 1971	Hond	2007	18 febr – 6 febr 2008	Zwijn